CHRISTMAS
FROM THE HEART
Volume 22

Meredith Consumer Marketing
Des Moines, Iowa

CHRISTMAS
FROM THE HEART

MEREDITH CORPORATION CONSUMER MARKETING
Vice President, Consumer Marketing: Janet Donnelly
Consumer Marketing Product Director: Heather Sorensen
Consumer Marketing Product Manager: Mary Ripperger
Business Director: Ron Clingman
Senior Production Manager: Al Rodruck
Photographers: Jay Wilde, Marty Baldwin, Jason Donnelly, Kritsada, Scott Little

WATERBURY PUBLICATIONS, INC.
Contributing Editor: Carol Field Dahlstrom
Contributing Illustrator: Chris Neubauer Graphics
Contributing Food Editor: Lois White
Contributing Food Stylists: Charles Worthington, Jennifer Peterson
Contributing Copy Editor: Terri Fredrickson
Contributing Proofreader: Gretchen Kauffman

Editorial Director: Lisa Kingsley
Creative Director: Ken Carlson
Associate Editors: Tricia Bergman, Mary Williams
Associate Design Director: Doug Samuelson
Production Assistant: Mindy Samuelson

BETTER HOMES AND GARDENS® MAGAZINE
Editor in Chief: Gayle Goodson Butler
Art Director: Michael D. Belknap
Senior Deputy Editor: Nancy Wall Hopkins
Editorial Assistant: Renee Irey

MEREDITH PUBLISHING GROUP
President: Tom Harty

MEREDITH CORPORATION
Chairman and Chief Executive Officer: Stephen M. Lacy

In Memoriam: E.T. Meredith III (1933–2003)

All of us at Meredith Consumer Marketing are dedicated to
providing you with information and ideas to enhance your home.
We welcome your comments and suggestions. Write to us at:
Meredith Consumer Marketing, 1716 Locust St., Des Moines, IA 50309-3023.

Contents

WE ALL LOVE A HANDMADE CHRISTMAS! You always make your own holiday ornaments, and you can't wait to bake Christmas cookies. You take time to craft those special gifts, and you feel so proud when you wrap that gift with a bow you made yourself.

Because you love a handmade Christmas (just like we do), we promise you'll love this book filled with ideas for creating wreaths, pillows, stockings, ornaments, tablescapes, treasured gifts, and so much more. You'll find table runners to quilt, table settings to make from paper, and purses made from felted sweaters. There are ideas for fresh centerpieces and beribboned mantel trims. You'll love the chapter that shares recipes for your favorite holiday sweets—cookies, bars, and cake pops—oh my! And the chapter on casseroles to share will come in handy for those Christmas parties and potluck gatherings.

May this holiday be happy and bright and filled with memories that will last a lifetime as you create a Christmas from the Heart.

The editors

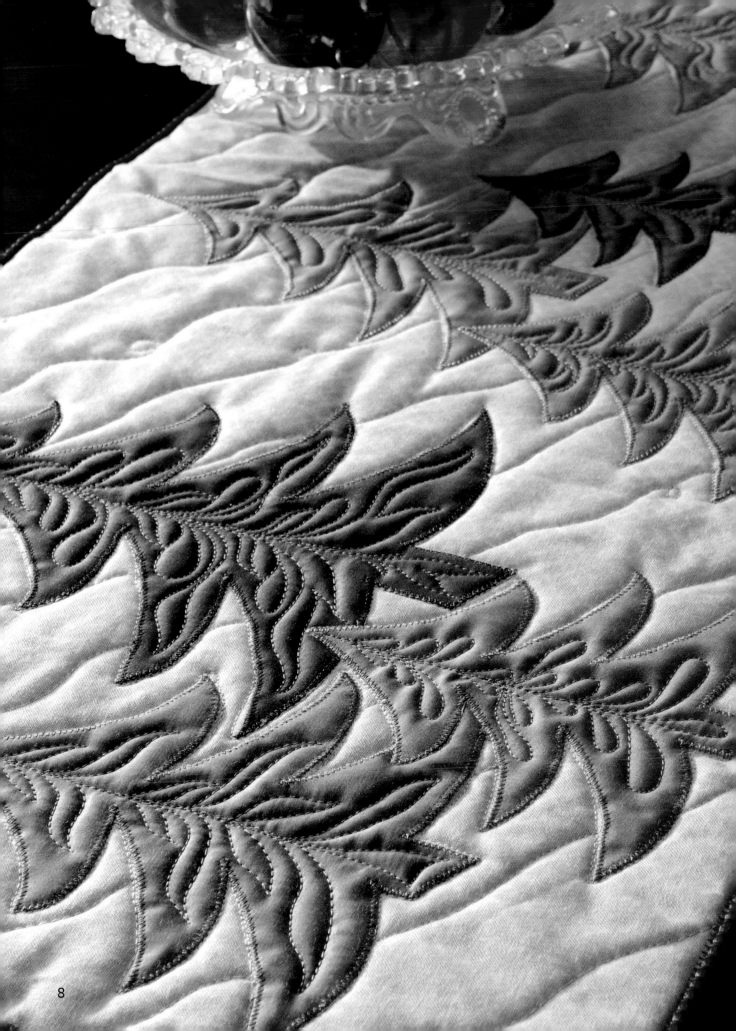

Tiny Tannenbaums

If one big evergreen tree can elicit wonder at Christmastime, why not spread the joy with multiple miniature evergreens? Whether the tiny trees are little real saplings or trees crafted from paper or fabric, let them make a big statement in this year's holiday decorating.

Tiny Tree Wreath

Tiny evergreen sprigs gather together into a floral foam wreath to make a stunning holiday wreath. Little felt balls are tucked in with the sprigs for a splash of color.

WHAT YOU NEED
Floral foam wreath • Princess club moss or other tiny evergreen sprig • Knife • Purchased small felt balls • 1-inch-wide apple green ribbon • Fine wire (optional)

WHAT YOU DO
1. Soak the floral foam until damp. Use the knife to make small slits in the floral foam. Push the sprigs into the foam wreath until the wreath is full.
2. Tuck the felt balls into the evergreen. Wire in place if necessary. Loop the ribbon around the top for hanging.

Green Apple Centerpiece

Tiny Princess club moss and green apples line up to make a natural centerpiece for your holiday table.

WHAT YOU NEED
Princess club moss or other tiny evergreen sprig • Green apple • Knife • Acorn tops • Twigs

WHAT YOU DO
Choose apples that have a flat bottom. Wash and polish the apples. Remove stem and use the knife to cut a hole at the stem. Insert the tiny sprig. Set on table and surround with acorn tops and twigs.

Paper Conifers

Tiny paper cones made from scrapbook papers and embellished with pom-poms and jewels are inverted to create a forest of paper trees.

WHAT YOU NEED

Tracing paper • Pencil • Patterned paper in a variety of coordinated colors/designs • Scissors • Adhesive, including strong double-sided tape and/or glue dots and foam dots • Decorative pom-pom ribbon • Embellishments, such as self-adhesive pearls or jewels

WHAT YOU DO

1. Trace tree patterns, opposite, onto tracing paper and cut out. Trace onto back side of patterned paper and cut out.

2. Shape the large tree pattern into a cone. Use strong tape adhesive and/or glue dots to secure.

3. Create an additional layer for some of the trees by making the smaller cone. Slip shorter cone onto tree and adhere in place using foam dots between layers.

4. Adhere decorative ribbon along the bottom edge of the top layer. Add self-adhesive jewels to trees for trim if desired.

Large Conifer
Full-Size Pattern

Small Conifer
Full-Size Pattern

Let nature inspire you to create a tablescape rich in texture and color. Combine the texture of tiny pinecones and monochromatic evergreen sprigs.

Egg Cup Table Favor

Silver egg cups showcase tiny juniper sprigs at each place setting.

WHAT YOU NEED

Silver egg cup • Water • Juniper sprigs • Tiny pinecones

WHAT YOU DO

Cut the juniper sprigs to fit the egg cup. Arrange the sprigs in the egg cup. Add a few drops of water. Surround with pinecones.

Mini Tree Tablescape

Foot-high yews, with root balls nestled in moss, look fresh when lined up in a galvanized tray. Anchor the trees with white and purple eggplants for an all-natural centerpiece. Achieve a similar look using a long dough bowl or low planter.

WHAT YOU NEED

Long galvanized tray, dough bowl, or other container • Moss (available at florists' shops or floral section of discount stores) • Purple and white eggplants • Greenery such as mint or lemon balm

WHAT YOU DO

Arrange the tiny yews with the root balls in a long tray. Fill in the tray with moss. Surround the trees with purple and white eggplants. Tuck other greenery around the eggplants.

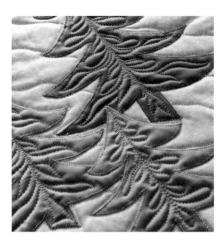

Little Forest Appliqué

Little bits of silk are cut in tree shapes and appliquéd to a creamy background to make an heirloom-quality quilted piece that can be used as a wall hanging or a table runner.

WHAT YOU NEED

Note: Amounts based on 40-inch-wide fabric

Fabrics

For Background: ½ yard cream/beige tone-on-tone print

For Appliqué: 1 fat quarter light green silk/cotton blend or cotton fabric • 1 fat quarter medium green silk/cotton blend or cotton fabric • 1 fat quarter dark green silk/cotton blend or cotton fabric

For Edging: 2½ yards dark red satin cording

1 yard paper-backed fusible web • ½ yard backing fabric • 14×26-inch piece of quilt batting

WHAT YOU DO

Cutting and Fusing the Fabrics

1. From the background fabric cut a 12×24-inch rectangle. Carefully iron out any folds or creases.

2. Enlarge and trace the following tree patterns, page 18, on the paper side of paper-backed fusible web:

1 Tree A; 2 Tree B; 1 Tree C; 2 Tree D; 3 Tree E

Note: The patterns are the reverse of the finished design.

3. Mark the pattern letter near one edge. Cut around the pattern pieces about ¼ inch outside the traced lines. If desired, remove the fusible web from the center of the pattern pieces by cutting about ¼ inch inside the traced line. This will give the finished trees a softer feel.

4. Referring to the paper-backed fusible web directions, fuse the tree patterns to the wrong side of the fabrics, making:

1 Tree B, 1 Tree D, and 1 Tree E from light green

1 Tree B, 1 Tree C, 1 Tree D, and 1 Tree E from medium green

1 Tree A and 1 Tree E from dark green

5. Cut out the trees on the traced lines.

Stitch the Appliqué

1. Remove paper backing and arrange trees in place on background rectangle, referring to the illustration, page 18, or as desired, keeping the tree tips at least ½ inch from the edges. Fuse in place.

2. Stitch around each tree with a small zigzag stitch (about 1.5 mm wide and 1 mm long) or a narrow satin zigzag stitch.

Finish the Quilt

1. Layer the quilt top, batting, and backing.

2. Quilt around each tree. Quilt inside each tree in a design that adds branch dimension. Quilt the background as desired.

3. Trim the top, excess batting, and backing to straighten the edges and square the corners. (See "Optional binding" for binding option rather than the edging directions below.)

4. With thread to match the cording, zigzag stitch (about 3 mm wide and 1 mm long) around the edge with the right zig of the stitch just over the edge of the fabric. Now stitch a row of the same-width satin stitches very close together; zigzag over the first round.

5. Starting at one corner, leaving about a 1-inch tail, lay the cording over the satin stitching on the edge of the quilt. Use a reverse hem stitch to stitch the cording on top of the satin stitching, slightly to the outside edge. As you come to the next corner, stitch just to the edge of the corner, leaving the needle down on the inside (left) edge. Turn the quilt and cording and continue stitching around to the start.

6. Trim the cording end to about 1 inch. Turn ends to the back and hand-stitch to the backing.

Note: Optional binding

For a traditional ¼-inch binding on finished piece, cut the background 12½×24½ inches. Purchase one fat quarter dark red silk/cotton blend or cotton fabric for binding. Cut five 2¼-inch strips from binding fabric. Join together with diagonal seams to make a continuous strip. Use to bind the quilt.

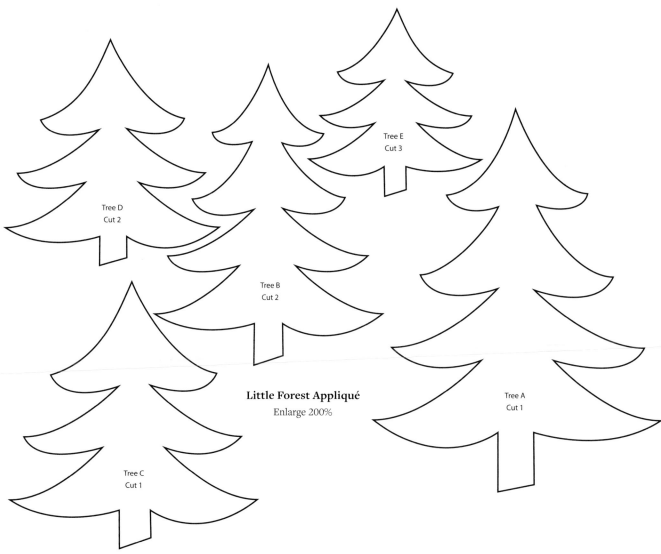

Tree E
Cut 3

Tree D
Cut 2

Tree B
Cut 2

Little Forest Appliqué
Enlarge 200%

Tree A
Cut 1

Tree C
Cut 1

Trees to Go

Searching for the perfect holiday table favor? Arborvitae seedlings planted in little tins make great take-home gifts.

WHAT YOU NEED
Small tin box (available at most scrapbook stores) • Scrapbook paper in desired color and pattern • Decorative scissors • Crafts glue • Stickers • Potting soil • Small tree seedling such as an arborvitae

WHAT YOU DO
Cut scrapbook paper strip to fit around the tin using decorative scissors. Print on the paper with computer generated words or use stickers. Wrap the tin with the paper and secure in the back with crafts glue. Add a sticker to the side of the box. Fill the decorated tin with potting soil and plant the tree.

EVERGREEN CARE TIPS

Some balled or potted decorative trees live long past the holidays. Plant them in the spring using these tips.

Pick Hardy Varieties. Check local nurseries for evergreen trees suited for your growing zone. (Norfolk Island pine is a houseplant; it can't survive outside.)

Take Care Over the Holidays. The air inside the house is very dry; so plants will dry out quickly. Place plants out of direct sun and water them about twice a week.

Minimize Display Time. The longer the trees are in the house, the more they'll begin to lose their hardiness. Limit indoor time to 2 to 3 weeks.

Cool Until Spring. After the holidays, store trees in an unheated, sheltered space, such as a garage with windows or a porch. Water once before storing, then leave them alone. Plant outside when the ground thaws.

Love the color, aroma, and texture of holiday greenery? Change it up a little by sharing a beautiful assortment of greenery in pretty pouches or vintage ironstone vessels.

In the Bag

This Christmas, greet guests with a tree at the front door instead of a wreath. A folded dish towel makes the pouch and shiny Christmas ornaments add the sparkle.

WHAT YOU NEED
Purchased dish towel • Needle and thread or sewing machine • Cheesecloth • Plastic bag • Red and green ribbon • Small Christmas ornaments • Small seedling such as Eastern white pine

WHAT YOU DO
With right sides together, fold the dish towel in half and stitch up both sides. Turn and press. Dampen the cheesecloth and wrap it around the bottom of the seedling. Tuck into the plastic bag. Tie the ribbons and ornaments around the bag about one-third from the top. Turn over the top of the bag. Use the ribbon to hang the bag.

Step-by-Step

Spell out holiday greetings on tree containers that climb the stairs. These paper letter ornaments offer a simple, decorative touch. The white ironstone pitchers and pots (mismatched but still complementary) were each planted with a lacy Goldcrest cypress tree.

WHAT YOU NEED
Mismatched ironstone pitchers or other containers • Paper letters printed from computer or stickers • Scrapbook paper • Scissors • Crafts glue • Masking tape • Ribbon • Potting soil • Small evergreen tree such as a Goldcrest cypress tree

WHAT YOU DO
1. Line up the pitchers or containers to plan the arrangement. Cut circles from scrapbook papers and layer as desired. Add computer-generated letters or stickers to the circles to spell a holiday message such as "JOY" or "NOEL" or other short word. Adhere a piece of ribbon to the back of the paper circle using masking tape. Set aside.
2. Fill each pitcher with potting soil and plant a tree. Tie a decorative letter around each pitcher. Arrange the pitchers or containers on steps or other flat surface.

Birdcage Beauty

Small-scale trees are all the rage. This petite juniper looks dapper in a vintage birdcage. Hang the cage from the ceiling or feature it on a tabletop.

WHAT YOU NEED
Small birdcage • Tiny potted tree • Small pinecones •
Artificial bird • Crafts glue • Ribbon

WHAT YOU DO
Place the potted tree inside the birdcage. Cover the bottom of the birdcage with pinecones. Slide the ribbon through the top of the birdcage for hanging. Glue the bird to the top of the cage.

China Cup Trees

Tiny trees are so charming, you don't even have to decorate them. Here, transferware ironstone bowls hold baby Norfolk Island pines. Tuck red pears around the trees for more Christmas color.

WHAT YOU NEED
Small vintage cups or bowls • Potting soil • Spoon •
Small tree such as a baby Norfolk Island pine • Acorns

WHAT YOU DO
With a spoon, place potting soil in a cup. Carefully plant the tiny trees. Gently add the acorns on top of the potting soil to cover the soil.

Tree in a Basket

Nuts of all kinds, with varied textures and shapes, make suitable ornaments for this tree in an apple-gathering basket.

WHAT YOU NEED

Container to hold the tree such as an apple basket • Small container to fit in basket such as a coffee can or jar • Water • Small evergreen tree • Newspapers • Flat rocks • Nuts in shells • Hot-glue gun and glue sticks • String

WHAT YOU DO

1. Place the tree in the small container and add water. Place tree and small container in basket. Stuff newspapers around the smaller container to fill space. Lay flat rocks on top of the newspapers.
2. Hot-glue small pieces of string to the nuts. Tie onto the tree.

Tree Topper Trio

Tops from spruce trees are placed in soil to make little evergreen groupings. Willow sticks bend around the toppers. Showcase the arrangements in maple syrup pails tied up with twine.

WHAT YOU NEED

Maple syrup containers or other outdoor containers • Potting soil • Spruce tree toppers • Willow branches • Berries on sticks • Twine • Pinecones

WHAT YOU DO

1. Fill the containers with potting soil. Push the tree toppers into the soil and arrange as desired. Bend the willow sticks and push into the soil to loop around the trees. Add berry pokes.
2. Tie twine and pinecones around the pails. Set on cut pieces of wood or other surfaces.

Sweet Decadence

Who doesn't love baked goods around Christmastime?
Get in on the pleasure of rolling and shaping cookie doughs,
layering bars, and creating fun new nibbles like cake pops. Every
sweet recipe crumbles into delicious bites of yumminess.

CHOCOLATE
PEPPERMINT

PEANUT
BUTTER CUP

CARROT CAKE

TIRAMISU

CHOCOLATE-
COVERED
CHERRY

Holiday Cake Pops

Arrange a bouquet of cute, cakey lollipops—each a scrumptious combo of crumbled cake and creamy frosting dipped in chocolaty candy coating.

WHAT YOU NEED

1   package 2-layer-size cake mix
1   to 1½ cups Basic Butter Frosting or desired variation*
12   ounces vanilla- or chocolate-flavor candy coating, chopped
34   to 36 lollipop sticks
12   ounces semisweet, dark, or white baking chocolate, chopped

WHAT YOU DO

1. Prepare desired-flavor cake mix according to package directions. Use any suggested pan size and bake according to package directions. Cool in pan on a wire rack. Line trays or baking sheets with waxed paper; set aside.
2. Remove cooled cake from pan and crumble into a very large mixing bowl. Add desired frosting. Beat with an electric mixer on low until combined. Using a small scoop, drop mixture into 1½-inch mounds onto prepared trays; roll mounds into balls and freeze for 30 minutes.
3. In a small microwave-safe dish heat 1 ounce of the coating (about ¼ cup) on 50% power (medium) for 60 seconds or until melted and smooth, stirring once. Dip one end of each lollipop stick into melted coating and poke sticks into balls (this helps the balls stay on the sticks). Freeze for 30 to 60 minutes more or until balls are firm.
4. Place remaining candy coating and chopped chocolate in a small saucepan. Heat over medium-low heat until melted and smooth, stirring frequently. Working in batches, dip balls into melted chocolate mixture. Allow excess to drip off; place balls on clean waxed paper-lined trays or baking sheets. (Poke ends of lollipop sticks into Styrofoam to suspend the pops until chocolate is set.) After coating is set, transfer balls to storage containers. Cover and store in the refrigerator for up to 1 week or in the freezer for up to

1 month. Let stand at room temperature at least 30 minutes before serving. Makes 34 to 36 cake pops.
Basic Butter Frosting: Beat ¼ cup softened butter with an electric mixer on medium until smooth. Gradually add ⅔ cup powdered sugar; beat well. Beat in 2 tablespoons milk and ½ teaspoon vanilla. Gradually beat in 2 cups powdered sugar. Beat in additional milk, 1 teaspoon at a time, to make frosting spreading consistency.
Almond Frosting: Prepare frosting as directed, except substitute ½ teaspoon almond extract for the vanilla.
Chocolate Frosting: Prepare frosting as directed, except substitute 2 tablespoons unsweetened cocoa powder for 2 tablespoons of the powdered sugar.
Coffee Frosting: Prepare frosting as directed, except add 1½ teaspoons instant espresso coffee powder or instant coffee crystals. Combine with the 2 tablespoons milk to dissolve before adding.
Lemon Frosting: Prepare frosting as directed, except substitute lemon juice for the milk and add ¼ teaspoon finely shredded lemon peel.
Peanut Butter Frosting: Prepare frosting as directed, except beat 2 tablespoons peanut butter into butter before adding powdered sugar.
Peppermint Frosting: Prepare frosting as directed, except substitute ⅛ teaspoon peppermint extract for the vanilla.
*Tip: If the higher amount of frosting is used, the cake balls will be rich and creamy but softer set. Make sure the balls are frozen solid and work quickly when dipping.

Cake Pop Creations

Pictured below and opposite.
Birthday Cake: Use confetti cake mix, Basic Butter Frosting, and vanilla-flavor candy coating and white baking chocolate for dipping. After dipping pops, sprinkle with 2 tablespoons confetti candies.

continued on next page

LEMON CREAM

BIRTHDAY CAKE

ULTIMATE CHOCOLATE

RED VELVET

COOKIES AND CREAM

COCONUT

continued from previous page

Carrot Cake: Use carrot cake mix, Basic Butter Frosting, and vanilla-flavor candy coating and white baking chocolate for dipping. After dipping pops, sprinkle with 1½ cups finely chopped toasted pecans.

Chocolate-Covered Cherry: Use chocolate cake mix, Almond Frosting, semisweet or dark chocolate, and chocolate-flavor candy coating for dipping. Before freezing the mounds of dough in Step 2, form each mound around a well-drained maraschino cherry.

Chocolate Peppermint: Use white cake mix, Peppermint Frosting, chocolate-flavor candy coating, and semisweet or dark chocolate for dipping. Stir 1 cup miniature semisweet baking pieces into crumbled cake. After dipping pops, sprinkle with ½ cup chopped peppermint candy.

Coconut: Use white cake mix, Basic Butter Frosting, and chocolate-flavor candy coating and semisweet or dark chocolate for dipping. Stir 1 cup toasted flaked coconut into crumbled cake. After dipping pops, sprinkle with additional 1 cup toasted flaked coconut.

Cookies and Cream: Use white cake mix, Basic Butter Frosting, and vanilla-flavor candy coating and white baking chocolate for dipping. Stir 1 cup crushed chocolate sandwich cookies with cream filling into crumbled cake. After dipping pops, sprinkle with ½ cup crushed chocolate wafer cookies.

Lemon Cream: Use lemon cake mix, Lemon Frosting, and vanilla-flavor candy coating and white baking chocolate for dipping. After dipping pops, sprinkle with ¼ cup finely crushed hard lemon candies (drops).

Peanut Butter Cup: Use chocolate cake mix, Peanut Butter Frosting, and chocolate-flavor candy coating and semisweet or dark chocolate for dipping. Stir 1 cup chopped chocolate-covered peanut butter cups into crumbled cake. After dipping pops, sprinkle with 1 cup finely chopped dry-roasted peanuts. Let dry and drizzle pops with melted chocolate.

Red Velvet: Use red velvet cake mix, Basic Butter Frosting, and vanilla-flavor candy coating and white baking chocolate for dipping. Reserve ½ cup crumbled cake. After dipping pops in white chocolate, sprinkle with reserved crumbled cake.

Tiramisu: Use yellow cake mix, Coffee Frosting, and vanilla-flavor candy coating and white baking chocolate for dipping. After dipping pops, top with chocolate-covered espresso beans. Let dry and drizzle pops with melted dark chocolate.

Ultimate Chocolate: Use devil's food chocolate cake mix, Chocolate Frosting, and chocolate-flavor candy coating and dark chocolate for dipping. After dipping pops, sprinkle with ¼ cup miniature semisweet baking pieces while chocolate is still wet.

Cherry-Almond Ornament Cookies

Embellish these pretty pink cutouts by piping on almond-flavor frosting and adding a maraschino cherry on top.

WHAT YOU NEED
30 to 36 maraschino cherries with stems
¾   cup butter, softened
¼   cup cream cheese, softened (2 ounces)
½   cup sugar
½   teaspoon almond extract
¼   teaspoon salt
2½ cups all-purpose flour
½   cup finely chopped candied cherries
1   recipe Cherry-Almond Frosting

WHAT YOU DO
1. Place maraschino cherries on paper towels to drain. Preheat oven to 325°F. Line a cookie sheet with parchment paper; set aside.
2. In a large bowl combine butter and cream cheese. Beat with an electric mixer on medium to high for 30 seconds. Add sugar, almond extract, and salt. Beat until combined, scraping sides of bowl occasionally. Beat in half of the flour just until combined. Beat in candied cherries and the remaining flour.
3. On a lightly floured surface roll dough to ½ inch thick. Using a 1½- to 2-inch fluted round cutter, cut out dough. Place cutouts 1 inch apart on prepared cookie sheet.
4. Bake for 14 to 15 minutes or until bottoms are light brown. Cool on cookie sheet for 2 minutes. Transfer to a wire rack; cool completely. Pipe or spoon Cherry-Almond Frosting onto cookie centers. Top each cookie with a maraschino cherry. Makes 30 to 36 cookies.

Cherry-Almond Frosting: In a medium bowl combine 3 ounces softened cream cheese and ¼ cup softened butter. Beat with an electric mixer on low for 30 seconds. Gradually beat in 2 cups powdered sugar. Beat in 1 tablespoon cherry liqueur or milk. Gradually beat in ½ to 1 cup additional powdered sugar to make frosting spreading consistency.

To Store: Layer unfrosted cookies between sheets of waxed paper in an airtight container. Store at room temperature for up to 3 days or freeze for up to 3 months. To serve, thaw cookies if frozen. Frost and top cookies as directed in Step 4.

Holiday Seven-Layer Bars

Baked in one big block, this simple, no-fuss bar satisfies every craving you have—sweet, chocolaty, nutty, and fruity.

WHAT YOU NEED

½ cup butter
2 cups finely crushed vanilla wafers (48 wafers) or shortbread cookies (33 cookies)
1 14-ounce can sweetened condensed milk
1 cup butterscotch-flavor pieces, candy-coated milk caramels (such as Sugar Babies), snipped vanilla caramels, semisweet chocolate pieces, or red and green candy-coated milk chocolate pieces
1 cup white baking pieces or one 6-ounce package white baking chocolate, chopped
1 cup mixed dried fruit bits, coarsely chopped dried apricots, golden raisins, dried cranberries, or dried cherries
1⅓ cups flaked or shredded coconut
1 cup unsalted mixed nuts or lightly salted roasted cashew pieces, coarsely chopped

WHAT YOU DO

1. Preheat oven to 350°F. Line a 13×9×2-inch baking pan with foil, extending the foil over the edges of the pan. Place butter in prepared pan; place in oven about 5 minutes or until butter melts. Tilt pan to coat bottom evenly. Sprinkle with crushed wafers.
2. Drizzle crust evenly with sweetened condensed milk. Sprinkle with butterscotch-flavor pieces, white baking pieces, fruit bits, coconut, and nuts. Press down firmly with the back of a spoon.
3. Bake for 25 minutes or until edges are lightly browned. Cool in pan on a wire rack. Use foil to lift baked mixture out of pan. Cut into bars. Makes 30 servings.
To Store: Place bars in a single layer in an airtight container. Cover and refrigerate for up to 3 days or freeze for up to 3 months.

Salted Chocolate-Caramel Rounds

For a mess-free counter, before you drizzle your cookies, place them on waxed paper or on a wire rack set over waxed paper. When you're done, just toss the waxed paper.

WHAT YOU NEED

2¾ cups all-purpose flour
¾ cup unsweetened cocoa powder
1 teaspoon baking soda
¼ teaspoon salt
1 cup butter, softened
1 cup granulated sugar
1 cup packed brown sugar
2 eggs
2 teaspoons vanilla

36 milk chocolate-covered round caramels
12 vanilla caramels, unwrapped
1 tablespoon whipping cream or half-and-half
 Coarse sea salt

WHAT YOU DO

1. In a medium bowl stir together flour, cocoa powder, baking soda, and the ¼ teaspoon salt; set aside.
2. In a large bowl beat butter with an electric mixer on medium to high for 30 seconds. Add granulated and brown sugars. Beat until combined, scraping bowl occasionally. Beat in eggs and vanilla until combined. Beat in as much of the flour mixture as you can with the mixer. Stir in any remaining flour mixture with a wooden spoon. If necessary, cover and chill dough for 1 hour or until dough is easy to handle.
3. Preheat oven to 375°F. Shape dough into 1½-inch balls. Press a chocolate-covered caramel into each ball and shape dough around caramel to enclose. Place cookies 2 inches apart on an ungreased cookie sheet.
4. Bake for 8 to 10 minutes or until edges are firm. Transfer cookies to a wire rack and cool completely.
5. To decorate, in a small saucepan combine vanilla caramels and whipping cream. Heat over medium-low heat until caramels melt and mixture is smooth. Drizzle melted caramel mixture over cookies and then sprinkle cookies with coarse sea salt. Let stand until set. Makes about 36 cookies.
To Store: Layer undecorated cookies between waxed paper in an airtight container. Cover and store at room temperature for up to 3 days or freeze for up to 3 months. To serve, thaw cookies if frozen. Drizzle cookies with caramel mixture and top with sea salt.

Four-Layer Nougat Bars

This outstanding no-bake treat features serendipitous layers of chocolate, butterscotch, caramel, and peanut butter. It's sure to become one of your new holiday favorites.

WHAT YOU NEED

1   12-ounce package (2 cups) semisweet chocolate pieces
1¼ cups butterscotch-flavor pieces
2   cups crisp rice cereal
1¼ cups sugar
⅓   cup butter
1   5-ounce can evaporated milk
1   7-ounce jar marshmallow creme
½   cup creamy peanut butter
1¾ cups cocktail peanuts or salted cashews, chopped
1   14-ounce package vanilla caramels, unwrapped

WHAT YOU DO

1. Line a 15×10×1-inch baking pan with foil, extending the foil over edges of pan. Lightly grease foil; set pan aside.

2. In a medium saucepan combine chocolate pieces and 1 cup of the butterscotch pieces. Cook and stir over medium-low heat until melted and combined. Transfer half of the mixture to a small saucepan; set aside.

3. For the base, stir rice cereal into remaining chocolate mixture. Immediately pour the chocolate-cereal mixture into the prepared baking pan. Using the back of a spoon or a thin offset spatula, spread mixture evenly in pan; press down to firmly pack mixture. Place pan in the freezer while preparing nougat layer.

4. For the nougat, in a medium saucepan combine sugar, butter, and ½ cup of the evaporated milk. Bring to boiling over medium-high heat; reduce heat to medium. Simmer, uncovered, for 5 minutes. Stir in the remaining ¼ cup butterscotch pieces until melted. Remove from heat. Stir in marshmallow creme and ¼ cup of the peanut butter until smooth. Stir in 1¾ cups chopped peanuts. Pour nougat over chilled base layer in the baking pan. Spread evenly to edges. Return pan to freezer while preparing caramel layer.

5. For caramel layer, in a large microwave-safe bowl combine caramels and the remaining evaporated milk (about 2 tablespoons). Microwave on high for 2 minutes or until melted, stirring every 30 seconds. Pour caramel layer evenly over nougat layer in pan, spreading evenly to edges. Return pan to freezer while preparing last layer.

6. Add the remaining ¼ cup peanut butter to the reserved chocolate-butterscotch mixture in the small saucepan. Cook and stir over medium-low heat until smooth. Pour mixture over caramel layer. Spread evenly to edges.

7. Cover and chill bars for 2 hours. Using the edges of the foil, lift uncut bars out of pan. Cut into bars. Makes 60 bars.

To Store: Place bars in a single layer in an airtight container. Cover and store in the refrigerator for up to 3 days.

Lining the pan with foil makes removing bars easier. Foil also helps keep pans from being damaged from knife cuts. Cleanup is a breeze.

Stained-Glass Snowflake Cookies

Crown your favorite cupcakes with snowflake cookies for a stunning holiday dessert.

WHAT YOU NEED

½ cup butter, softened
½ cup sugar
¼ teaspoon salt
1 egg
1½ teaspoons light-color corn syrup
1 teaspoon finely shredded lemon peel
1 teaspoon lemon extract
1¾ cups all-purpose flour
3 ounces assorted fruit-flavor hard candy
1 recipe Royal Icing (recipe, page 38)
   White decorative candies or sprinkles

WHAT YOU DO

1. In a large mixing bowl beat butter with an electric mixer on medium to high for 30 seconds. Add sugar and salt. Beat until combined, scraping bowl occasionally. Beat in egg, corn syrup, lemon peel, and lemon extract until combined. Beat in as much of the flour as you can with the mixer. Stir in any remaining flour with a wooden spoon. Divide dough in half. If necessary, cover and chill dough about 30 minutes or until easy to handle.

2. Preheat oven to 375°F. On a lightly floured surface roll half of the dough at a time to ⅛-inch thickness. Using floured snowflake cookie cutters, cut snowflakes in assorted sizes. Place cutouts 1 inch apart on a foil-lined cookie sheet. Using smaller cutters, cut shapes out of snowflake cookie centers. Reroll trimmings for additional cutouts.

3. Separate hard candies by color. Place each color in a small, heavy resealable plastic bag; seal bag. Using a meat mallet, finely crush candy. Spoon some of the crushed candy into each center cutout, completely filling to the same thickness as cookies.

4. Bake for 7 to 8 minutes or until edges are firm and bottoms are very lightly browned. Transfer cookie sheet to a wire rack; let cookies cool. Using a thin metal spatula, carefully peel foil from backs of cookies.

5. Frost cookies with Royal Icing and decorate with candies or sprinkles. Makes 2 to 3 dozen cookies.

To Store: Layer undecorated cookies between waxed paper in an airtight container. Cover and store at room temperature for up to 3 days or freeze for up to 3 months. To serve, thaw cookies if frozen. Frost and decorate.

Festive Thumbprints

WHAT YOU NEED

⅔ cup butter, softened
½ cup granulated sugar
2 egg yolks
1 teaspoon vanilla
½ teaspoon mint extract

1½ cups all-purpose flour
   Coarse red or green sugar
15 red candy coating disks
15 green candy coating disks

WHAT YOU DO

1. In a large mixing bowl beat butter with an electric mixer on medium to high for 30 seconds. Add granulated sugar. Beat until combined, scraping bowl occasionally. Beat in egg yolks, vanilla, and mint extract. Beat in as much of the flour as you can. Stir in any remaining flour. Cover and chill dough about 1 hour or until easy to handle.

2. Preheat oven to 375°F. Shape dough into 1-inch balls. Roll balls in coarse sugar. Place 1 inch apart on cookie sheets. Press your thumb into the center of each ball. Bake for 10 to 12 minutes or until bottoms are lightly browned. If cookie centers have puffed up during baking, repress with the rounded side of a measuring teaspoon. Immediately after baking, place candy disks in the center of the cookies. Transfer cookies to a wire rack; let cool. Makes 30 cookies.

To Store: Layer cookies between waxed paper in an airtight container. Cover and store at room temperature for up to 3 days or freeze for up to 3 months.

Reindeer Cookie Cutouts

If you plan to hang the reindeer cookies, as shown on page 27, use a drinking straw to make holes in cutouts before baking. If a hole bakes shut, remake the hole as soon as the cookie comes out of the oven.

WHAT YOU NEED
⅔ cup butter, softened
¾ cup granulated sugar
1 teaspoon baking powder
¼ teaspoon salt
1 egg
1 tablespoon milk
1 teaspoon vanilla
2 cups all-purpose flour
1 recipe Royal Icing

WHAT YOU DO
1. In a large mixing bowl beat butter with an electric mixer on medium to high for 30 seconds. Add granulated sugar, baking powder, and salt. Beat until combined, scraping bowl occasionally. Beat in egg, milk, and vanilla until combined. Beat in as much of the flour as you can with the mixer. Stir in any remaining flour. Divide dough in half. Cover and chill for 1 to 2 hours or until dough is easy to handle.
2. Preheat oven to 375°F. On a lightly floured surface roll half of the dough at a time to ⅛- to ¼-inch thickness. Using a floured 6×5-inch reindeer-shape cookie cutter, cut out dough. Place cutouts 1 inch apart on ungreased cookie sheets.
3. Bake for 7 to 10 minutes or until edges are firm and bottoms are very lightly browned. Transfer cookies to a wire rack and let cool. Makes 12 cookies.

Decorating Options: Frost cutouts with white, red-, or green-tinted Royal Icing. Then apply one of these creative decorating techniques:
• Gold or silver gilding: Pipe designs onto the hardened base coat and let it dry. Brush the raised designs with a luster dust and vodka mixture. (Vodka is used because it evaporates and dries quickly.)
• Marbling: Swirl white icing into a still-wet base of green-tinted icing. Let the marbled icing dry and harden.
• Progressive piping: Pipe rows of dots on the hardened basecoat.
• Freeform designs: Outline cookie edges with icing after basecoat has hardened. Add simple designs.
To Store: Layer undecorated cookies in a single layer in an airtight container. Cover and store at room temperature for up to 3 days or freeze for up to 3 months.

Royal Icing

WHAT YOU NEED
1 16-ounce package powdered sugar
3 tablespoons meringue powder
½ teaspoon cream of tartar
½ cup warm water
1 teaspoon vanilla

WHAT YOU DO
1. In a large mixing bowl stir together powdered sugar, meringue powder, and cream of tartar. Add the warm water and vanilla. Beat with an electric mixer on low until combined; beat on high for 7 to 10 minutes or until icing is very stiff. If not using right away, cover bowl with a damp paper towel and cover paper towel with plastic wrap; chill for up to 48 hours. Makes about 5 cups.

Embellish other cutout cookies using the same Royal Icing and decorating techniques to create something memorable for the holiday season.

Beautifully Beribboned

Let the beautiful textures and colors of ribbon help you decorate for Christmas this year. Combine ribbons in colors, textures, and patterns that you love to create vibrant holiday decorations brimming with seasonal style.

By the roll or by the yard, choose ribbons in colors to accent your holiday decorating scheme. Add lengths of ribbon to wreaths or drape yards of ribbon on mantels for striking color accents.

Peppermint and Orange Wreath

Sliced and dried oranges and peppermint sticks are layered on a foam wreath and adorned with a cascade of ribbon for this fresh-look holiday wreath.

WHAT YOU NEED
Foam wreath form (available at crafts stores) • Sliced and dried oranges (available at crafts stores or can dry your own) • Peppermint sticks • Hot-glue gun and glue sticks • 1-inch-wide ribbon in desired colors • Rock candy sticks • Greenery • Scissors

WHAT YOU DO
1. Plan the arrangement on the wreath form using the dried oranges and peppermint sticks. Hot-glue to the foam wreath form, overlapping the oranges to cover the foam.
2. Cut lengths of ribbon and glue to the top of the wreath. Tie a bow and glue over the ribbon strips. Glue rock candy at the top behind the ribbon. Tuck greenery into ribbons.

Draped Ribbon Mantel Trim

Add a graceful accent to mantels or windows with wide wired ribbons.

To hang ribbons, insert evenly spaced pushpins or wire nails into the top of a mantel or window frame. Drape one color of wired ribbon across the surface, wrapping around the nails or pins. Allow the ribbon to drape to a depth of about one-half the length from nail to nail. Repeat with other colors.

Instead of the traditional red and green at Christmastime, combine variations of these familiar favorites. Choose fuchsia red, pretty purple, and apple green for a fun and unexpected holiday combination.

Fit to Be Tied

Choose colors of ribbon that fit your holiday color scheme and then wrap bands of wide ribbon around your packages. Finish with ribbon bows in multiple sizes and patterns to give paper wrap a happy jolt of color.

Ribbon-Wrapped Votives

Turn simple glass votives into mini works of art with alternating strips of ribbon. The light from the candles inside will showcase the beautiful colors you choose.

WHAT YOU NEED

Glass votive candle holders • Decoupage medium • Paintbrush • Scraps of ribbon in desired colors

WHAT YOU DO

Be sure the glass candle holders are clean and dry. Plan the design first. Use the paintbrush to paint a coat of decoupage medium on the outside of the glass votive as you work on small sections at a time. Add alternating strips of ribbon, layering ribbons as desired. Let dry.

Foursome Ribbon Wreath

When one ribbon bow is so pretty, why not make even more? Decorate a fresh evergreen wreath with a foursome of beautiful tied satin bows for a stunning holiday wreath.

WHAT YOU NEED
Fresh green wreath • 1½ yards of 1½-inch-wide satin ribbon for each bow • Fine wire • Double-sided tape

WHAT YOU DO
1. Cut the following lengths of ribbon for each bow: one 11-inch piece, two 15-inch pieces, one 3½-inch piece.
2. Loop the 11 inch-piece of ribbon at both ends bringing the ends to the middle. Secure with double-sided tape.
3. Crisscross the 15-inch pieces, making an X. Lay the looped ribbon in the center of the X and secure with wire in the back.
4. Fold the long sides of the 3½-inch piece of ribbon to the middle. Wrap it around the center of the looped ribbon to cover the wire.
5. Make four bows total. Wrap the crisscross part of the ribbon around the wreath at top and bottom and sides.

Eye Candy

Snippets of ribbon in rich, saturated colors wind around foam candy cane shapes that look good enough to eat—and are a cinch to make!

WHAT YOU NEED
Plastic foam candy cane shapes (available at crafts stores) • ⅜-inch-wide ribbon in desired color and pattern • ⅛-inch-wide ribbon in desired color and pattern • Glue suitable for plastic foam, such as Floracraft glue • Crafts glue • Double-sided adhesive • Scissors

WHAT YOU DO
1. Wind the ⅜-inch ribbon around foam candy cane shapes, securing with foam glue at the beginning and end. Be sure to leave some of the white of the cane showing to resemble a candy cane.
2. To finish, use double-sided adhesive to attach a ⅛-inch ribbon in a contrasting color and style over the first ribbon. Secure at the end with crafts glue.

Patterned Paper-Ribbon Wraps

Patterned paper tape ribbon is a wonderful way to create your own ribbon magic. You can overlap it, make designs with it, and even reposition it. Have fun wrapping your gifts this year with this fun craft ribbon.

WHAT YOU NEED
Patterned paper tape in assorted colors and patterns such as Washi tape • Wrapped package • Stickers, jewels, and other embellishments • Gift tag (optional)

WHAT YOU DO
Plan the design before you begin. Layer the tape on the packages, overlapping and weaving as desired. Add embellishments on or beside the tape. Add a gift tag if desired.

Patterned Paper-Ribbon Vases

Paper tape ribbon works well on paper, but it also works well on glass. Dress up clear glass vessels with some overlapped tape and then fill them with holiday ornaments or candy.

WHAT YOU NEED
Patterned paper tape in assorted colors and patterns such as Washi tape • Clear glass vessel or vase with straight sides • Vinegar • Adhesive jewels

WHAT YOU DO
Be sure the glass is clean and dry. Wipe off with vinegar and let dry completely. Plan the design before you begin. Layer the tape on sides of the glass vase, overlapping the tape to make new patterns. Place jewels on tape.

TWO-TONE
BOW

FLORAL
BOW

TIERED
BOW

TAILORED
BOW

DIOR
BOW

CLASSIC
BOW

Bow Know-How

You have searched for the perfect gift for everyone on your Christmas list. Presenting the gift is just as much fun when you tie it up using the perfect bow. Whether you want to make a floral-style bow or a tailored variety, choose the ribbons that you love and then follow these steps to make the perfect bow.

Tiered Bow

WHAT YOU DO

1. Use three widths and three types of ribbon to fashion this bow. Cut the widest ribbon the longest, the narrowest ribbon the shortest, and the remaining ribbon a length in between. Notch the ends. Tie the stacked lengths in the center with another piece of ribbon, leaving long tails.
2. Trim and conceal the ribbon tails or use the tails to secure the bow to the package.

Dior Bow

WHAT YOU DO

1. Cut four pieces of ribbon in graduating lengths. Form the pieces into loops and secure with glue. Flatten and secure the three largest loops in the center with glue. Stack all four pieces, adhering them together in the center with glue.
2. Cut another piece of ribbon. Wrap it around the center of the bow through the top loop.
3. Trim and secure the ends of the wrapped ribbon on the back of the bow.

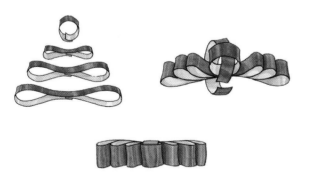

Two-Tone Bow

WHAT YOU DO

1. Choose two ribbons—one wider than the other—for your bow. Cut both ribbons twice the desired length of the finished bow. Form the wider piece into a loop and secure with glue. Center and wrap the narrower piece around the first and secure.
2. Flatten the layered loop and secure in the center with glue. Cut another piece of ribbon; wrap and tie it around the center of the flattened loop.
3. Pull the tails of the wrapped ribbon tight, trim the ends, and secure on the back of the bow with glue.

Tailored Bow

WHAT YOU DO

1. Cut a piece of ribbon twice the desired length of the finished bow. Form the piece into a loop and secure with glue. Flatten the loop and secure in the center with glue. Cut another piece of ribbon and wrap it around the center.
2. Glue the ends of the wrapped center to the back of the finished bow.

continued on next page

continued from previous page

What fun to wrap those special gifts with beautiful ribbon. But it is the beautiful bow that is the center of attention on most gifts tucked under the Christmas tree! Choose the bow that suits your style and wrap it up!

Classic Bow

WHAT YOU DO

1. Being careful not to twist the ribbon, fold the ribbon length back and forth, forming two loops at the top and one loop in the bottom center.
2. Cross the top left loop over the top right loop.
3. Fold the left loop down behind the right loop and then through the bottom loop.
4. Pull the top loops taut, forming a knot in the center of the bow. Trim the tails and notch the ends.

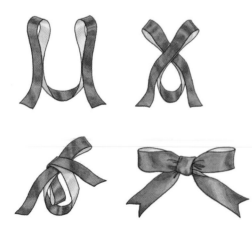

Floral Bow

WHAT YOU DO

1. Determine the tail length for your bow and twist the ribbon at this point, keeping the right side of the ribbon facing you.
2. Make a loop and give the ribbon a twist. Holding the twist between your thumb and index finger, make a second loop the same size in the opposite direction. Twist the loop toward you.
3. Continue making same-size loops in this way until the bow has the fullness you want. Wrap a narrow width of ribbon around the bow center, tying the tails together in the back of the bow. Do not trim the narrow ribbon tails.
4. Arrange the loops as desired to shape your bow. Use the narrow ribbon tails to attach the bow to your package.

**Patterned Paper-Ribbon
Ornament**
Full-Size Patterns

Patterned Paper-Ribbon Ornaments

*Add a little color and texture to clear glass balls with patterned
paper tape and some jingle bells and holly leaves.*

WHAT YOU NEED

Clear glass ornaments • Patterned paper tape in
assorted colors and patterns such as Washi tape •
Scissors • Green scrapbook paper scraps • Double-sided
adhesive tape • Red adhesive jewels • 5 or 6 small red,
gold, and green jingle bells • Narrow ribbon

WHAT YOU DO

1. Be sure the ornaments are clean and dry. Plan the design
before you start. If the tape is too wide for the ornament
size, cut the tape in half lengthwise. Wrap tape around the
ornament.
2. Trace the patterns, above, and cut out. Draw around the
patterns on the green scrapbook paper and cut out. Use
the tape to secure the leaves to the front of the ornament.
Add the jewels on top of the leaves.
3. Remove the top of the ornament and add the jingle bells.
Replace the top and add a ribbon for hanging.

In Full Bloom

Whether you prefer poinsettias, amaryllis, tulips, or daisies—flowers at Christmastime make the season bright! So create festive and fresh arrangements in shades of red, white, and green to add bright notes of holiday merriment.

An amaryllis bloom is a stunning display of color and shape all by itself. Displayed with vintage ornaments or dusted with silvery glitter, these blooms are an elegant yet simple way to decorate for the holidays.

Pitcher of Blooms

After your potted amaryllis has bloomed, cut it off and place in a vase of water. With a little magic you can surround it with vintage ornaments.

WHAT YOU NEED
Large clear glass pitcher or other glass container • Smaller vase to fit inside the larger one • Small ornaments • Water • Cut amaryllis stem

WHAT YOU DO
Referring to the diagram, below, put the smaller vase inside the larger one. Place small ornaments between the two glass containers. Fill the smaller vase with water. Put the cut amaryllis stem in the small vase.

Glittering Amaryllis

For a simple yet stunning centerpiece or table favor, cut a pink amaryllis bloom and place in a clear dish of water. Sprinkle glitter over the top of the bloom, letting the glitter pool in the natural crevices of the flower.

Keep it simple by choosing unexpected containers for your pretty flowers. Whether placed in vintage pewter pitchers or fun-filled boots, your blooms will say "Merry Christmas!"

Shiny and Bright Blooms

Vintage pewter containers combine with shiny ornaments to make a stunning holiday centerpiece.

WHAT YOU NEED

Vintage pitchers or containers • Water • Silver tray • Silver ornaments • White flowers such as daisies and baby's breath

WHAT YOU DO

Set the containers on the silver tray and fill container with water. Arrange the white flowers in the containers. Surround the containers with silver ornaments.

Pretty in Pink Poinsettias

Everyone loves poinsettias at Christmastime. This year, think pink by presenting the pretty poinsettias in pink vinyl boots that welcome guests at the doorway.

WHAT YOU NEED

Pink or red vinyl boots • Narrow, tall vases or jars to fit inside the boots • Thin white branches • Cut poinsettia stems

WHAT YOU DO

Be sure the boots are clean and dry. Set the jars in the boots and fill with water. Add the stems to the jar of water. Tuck the branches into the boots.

Add some holiday shimmer and shine to your Christmas floral arrangements with a small gazing ball or candles to accompany a grouping of blooms.

Roses and Gazing Ball

A holiday-red gazing ball is placed in a large wide vase and surrounded with roses for a brilliant table arrangement.

WHAT YOU NEED
Large clear glass vase with wide top • Small red gazing ball • Floral tacky wax • Water • Fresh red or pink roses • Fresh greenery

WHAT YOU DO
Be sure the vase is clean and dry. Secure the gazing ball in the bottom of the vase using the tacky wax. Add water. Cut the roses, leaving stems about 4 inches long or just long enough to reach the water. Place them all around the ball. Add fresh greenery.

Candles in Bloom

Lime green amaryllis blooms are cut and tucked into a vintage glass bowl of the same color. Green votive candles are snuggled among the blooms to make a warm and inviting centerpiece.

Never leave a burning candle unattended.

Boxed Florals

Poinsettia bracts, ranunculus, and amaryllis burst from a vase like tissue paper from a box. Fit a ceramic cube with wet floral foam or crumbled chicken wire. Then tuck in stems and magnolia leaves for a look that's full but loose.

Blooming Ornaments

Tiny blooms pop out of ornaments to make cheerful decorations for your holiday table. Perch them on clear candlestick holders and set them at each place setting.

WHAT YOU NEED
Ball ornament • Water • Cut blooms • Fresh greenery • Clear glass candlestick holder • Narrow ribbon

WHAT YOU DO
Remove the top from the ornament and set aside. Place the ornament on the candlestick and fill half full with water. Place the bloom in the ornament. Add a sprig of fresh greenery. Tie a ribbon around the top of the ornament.

Holiday Topiary

This stunning amaryllis bloom arrangement will last for days and bring festive cheer to any table or mantel.

WHAT YOU NEED

Large tall container • Floral foam • Water • Cardboard tube • Wrapping paper • Scissors • Cut amaryllis • Sprigs of evergreen, holly, or ivy

WHAT YOU DO

1. Be sure the container is clean and dry. Soak floral foam in water until it is saturated and then cut it to fit your container.

2. Cover a cardboard tube with wrapping paper, cutting the paper about 2 inches shorter than the tube. Push the tube 2 inches into the florist's foam.

3. Cut the amaryllis stems long enough to reach down through the tube and penetrate the foam, with the flowers resting at the top of the tube.

4. Add snippets of evergreen, holly, or ivy around the rim of the vase; the arrangement will stay fresh in the foam for about 1 week.

THE AMAZING AMARYLLIS

Even though we may think of the poinsettia as the most common Christmas bloom, the amaryllis is its close second. Known for its beautiful Christmas-red color, it also comes in pink, white, and lime green. Growing the bloom is fun—watching it come from an onionlike bulb into a princesslike bloom. Here are some tips on growing your amaryllis:

Choose the right bulb. Choose a healthy bulb; they may be green or they may be covered with crisp brown skin, a little like an onion bulb with a tuft of roots at the base. Select a pot that's slightly larger than the bulb and that has a drainage hole. Put a handful of potting soil in the bottom of the pot and place the bulb on top. The neck and shoulders of the bulb should show above the rim of the pot. Fill in around it with potting soil, tapping it a little to settle the bulb into the pot.

How to Care for Your Amaryllis

Water well. Allow water to drain through the pot and make sure the water stays below the top of the bulb. Place the pot in a sunny spot. Water sparingly until a flower spike appears. Soil should be moist but never soggy.

Keep the pot warm. Amaryllis are touchy about cool breezes. Put the pot in a draft-free spot. Wait patiently. Most amaryllis will bloom four to six weeks after planting.

Move flowers. Once flowers start to open, indirect light is best. Snip off flowers as they fade. Cut the stems about 1 inch from the base after all flowers have bloomed. Strappy leaves brown as the flowering period ends.

Good to Know

Amaryllis like to be pot-bound, so a container only 1 inch or so larger than the bulb is just right. Any pot will do, as long as it has a hole for drainage. Terra-cotta pots are good choices because they are porous and their weight helps stabilize the plants, which grow quite tall. Lay bits of sheet moss (available at garden shops) on top of the soil to help conserve moisture and create a woodsy and natural look. Or plant a sprig of variegated ivy around the edge and tuck a Christmas ornament or two in next to the bulb. The biggest bulbs may send up as many as four flower spikes during one season.

It only takes a few minutes to make a topiary arrangement with cut amaryllis in a pedestal vase. Keeping the long, top-heavy stem of beautiful blooms upright is easy when you use a cardboard tube wrapped in pretty wrapping paper.

All That Glitters

Make your Christmas sparkle this year by creating magical
holiday decor with razzle-dazzle baubles, sparkling glitter,
metallic paints, shimmering jewels, and golden ribbons.

Metallic Leaf Ornaments

Using the beauty of nature and a little sparkling paint, these elegant leaf ornaments make Mother Nature the star.

WHAT YOU NEED

Natural leaves • Gold and silver metallic spray paint • Metallic spray paints in red, yellow, green, purple, and blue (we used model car hobby paints found at hobby and crafts stores) • Newspapers • Crafts glue • Gold or natural raffia

WHAT YOU DO

1. To press the leaves for painting, lay the leaves under a heavy weight such as a book and dry overnight. Choose leaves that are dry but not too crisp or brittle.

2. Lay the leaves on newspaper. Spray with gold or silver spray paint. Let dry. Turn and spray the other side. Let dry. The gold or silver becomes the base coat for the leaves.

3. Add another color of spray paint over the gold or silver. Very lightly spray the desired color over the gold or silver, letting the base color show through slightly.

4. Tie or glue a generous piece of raffia to the stem for a bow.

Copper and Candle Centerpiece

Copper cookie cutters reflect the candlelight to make a shimmering centerpiece.

WHAT YOU NEED

Copper cookie cutters in desired shapes • Votive candles to fit in the cookie cutters • Long ceramic or glass plate or platter • Copper-trimmed ribbon

WHAT YOU DO

Place the cookie cutters on the tray or plate. Place the candles in the cutters, slicing off bits of the bottom edges if necessary to fit. Wind the ribbon around the edges of the cookies cutters on the plate.

Never leave a burning candle unattended.

Glitter Birdies

A foam ball in the hand quickly becomes four glitter birds on the tree with just a little glitter and a few feathers.

WHAT YOU NEED

4-inch plastic foam ball, such as Styrofoam • Silver glitter paint • Silver glitter • Glitter craft foam sheet • Straight pins • Black mini brads • 18-gauge wire (or spiraled paper clip) • Feathers • Glue suitable for plastic foam, such as Floracraft glue • Black paper scraps • Single-pronged hair clip • Silver glitter chenille stem • Serrated knife • Wire cutters • Paintbrush • Hot-glue gun and glue sticks

WHAT YOU DO

1. Using a serrated knife, carefully cut the plastic foam ball in half using a gentle back and forth sawing action. Next cut each half in half again, similar to cutting an apple into quarters. Each quarter will become a bird. Working with one section at a time, use scissors to snip ¼ inch off one pointed end. Leave the other end intact. This makes the point for the tail.

2. Working over a protected surface with one section at a time, cover the foam with glitter paint. While the paint is wet, sprinkle silver glitter over the paint. Let the paint dry completely.

3. Use the pattern, right, as your guide to cut two wings out of the glitter foam for each bird. Apply foam glue to the underside of the wings and glue them to each side of the bird's back. Anchor each wing in place with a straight pin. Poke a feather end into the pointed tail end. Stabilize the tail with a dot of foam glue.

4. If you're using a spiraled paper clip, simply cut it in half with wire cutters. If you're using wire, spiral the end and then cut the finished spiral off the wire coil. Poke the flat wire end into the top of the head (rounded end of the section). Add a small amount of foam glue to strengthen the insertion. Push the brad eyes into each side of the head below the wire spiral.

5. To make the beak, fold the black paper in half and cut out two small triangles. Hot-glue a straight pin head between the paper triangles. Poke the finished beak into the head.

6. Attach the hangers by cutting a 2-inch section of chenille stem for each bird. Fold each 2-inch chenille section in half. Working on one section at a time, open a hair clip and thread the chenille ends out the top of two holes in the metal. Poke the chenille ends up into the underside of the finished bird. Squeeze foam glue up into the connection. Reinforce the bird connection by adding a little hot glue between the metal and glittered underside. **Note:** Use caution; if the hot glue touches the plastic foam, the foam will melt.

Glitter Bird Wing
Full-Size Pattern

Jeweled Monogram

Transform a plain alphabet letter into a work of art with jewels and beads.

WHAT YOU NEED

Green acrylic paint • Wood or plaster alphabet letter • Vintage or new pins and jewels • Microbeads • Assorted beads in desired colors • Crafts glue

WHAT YOU DO

1. Paint the letter with acrylic paint. Let dry.
2. Working in sections, spread the glue onto the letter. Press in jewels, beads, or vintage pieces. For small areas sprinkle microbeads over the glue to cover the letter completely. Let dry.

Simple chenille stems magically turn into glittering stars to adorn any Christmas tree. A purchased faux pearl spray winds into a stunning wreath for holiday sparkle.

Silver Chenille Star

Already feathered with metallic sheen, silver chenille stems just need a little twist to become enchanting snowflakes.

WHAT YOU NEED

Silver chenille stems • Hot-glue gun and glue sticks

WHAT YOU DO

Plan your design first. Lay the chenille stems on a flat surface to straighten. Form the desired star shape. Seal the ends with hot glue to keep the shape from unwinding.

Blue Christmas Wreath

A faux-pearl spray cut into strips makes a sparkling wreath in just a few minutes.

WHAT YOU NEED

Faux pearl spray • Wire cutters • Hot-glue gun and glue sticks • Ribbon with metallic edge • Scissors

WHAT YOU DO

Cut faux pearl spray into lengths and twist the strips together. Wind the strip into a circle to form wreath. Hot-glue to secure the ends. Tie a bow with the ribbon and hot-glue to the top of the wreath.

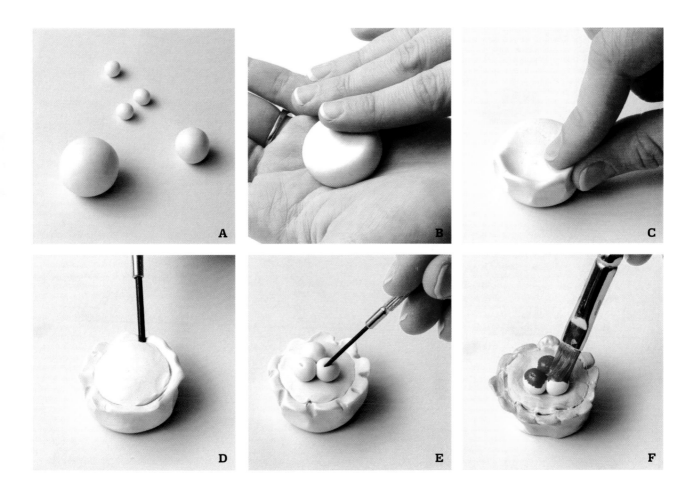

Sugar Candy Ornaments

Polymer clay is transformed into sugar candy and boxed up to make the sweetest of ornaments.

WHAT YOU NEED
Polymer clay such as Sculpey • Acrylic paint in desired colors for candy • Acrylic gold metallic paint for box • Small screwdriver • Needle • Small cardboard box • Ribbon • Glitter • Small piece of cardboard • Crafts glue

WHAT YOU DO
1. To make the candy, start with ball about 1 inch in diameter of the base piece. Make other little balls for the details on the candy. See Photo A.
2. For the tiny candy with crust, flatten the ball gently between palms of hands so the ball is just a bit flatter. See Photo B. Using finger and thumb, pinch to bring sides in and up all the way around "crust." See Photo C.

3. Flatten a medium-size circle to make a tiny pancake shape. Lay on top of piecrust. Use small screwdriver tool to make piecrust grooves all around the top. Use tip of finger to further shape scallops of piecrust as desired. See Photo D.
4. Make circle outline around filling using small screwdriver or a needle. Make little round balls and arrange on top for berries. See Photo E.
5. Bake at 275°F for 20 to 30 minutes or follow directions on the box of polymer clay. Let cool.
6. Paint the little candies as desired, letting the colors dry before moving on to next color. Dust with glitter. Let dry.
7. Cut two pieces of cardboard to fit inside the box to form the candy sections. Glue to inside of box. Paint with gold paint. Let dry.
8. Glue the candies inside the box. Add a ribbon at the corner for hanging.

Silvery Jute Trees

Nothing could be easier than coiling jute around a foam cone. Once the cone is completely encased in jute, a blast of silver and glitter spray paints transforms the rustic tree into an elegant centerpiece. The wire star tree topper features a metallic bead that blends beautifully with the tree base.

WHAT YOU NEED

Plastic foam cone such as Styrofoam • Jute string • Stove pipe wire • Oversize ceramic beads • Straight pins • Floral glue such as Floracraft • Silver spray paint and silver glitter paint such as Krylon • Hot-glue gun and glue sticks

WHAT YOU DO

1. Apply glue to the bottom few inches of the cone. Working from the spool of jute, use a straight pin to anchor the jute end to the bottom of the plastic foam cone. Start wrapping the jute around the cone. Make sure each wrap lies directly on top of the wrap below it. Whenever necessary, use straight pins to hold the jute in place. Once the glue area is covered, apply more glue and continue wrapping. Once you reach the top of the cone, cut the jute off the spool. Apply glue to the very top and spiral the end of the jute over the glue. Use a pin to anchor the jute end to the cone top. Let the jute-covered cone dry overnight.

2. Working in a well-ventilated area over a protected surface, spray paint the jute silver. Rotate the tree to make sure you've covered all sides of the cone. **Note:** Do not spray the uncovered base because spray paint destroys the plastic foam. A quick overcoat of glitter spray paint will add sparkle to the tree.

3. Cut off a 2-foot length of wire. Hook a bead onto one end of the wire, encircling the wire around the bead. When you return to where the wire came out of the bead, switch directions. While working the wire back around in the circle, use pliers to bend the wire at ½-inch intervals to make a five-point star. After the final point, bring the wire down, leaving a 2-inch tail to insert into the top off the cone. Trim off the excess wire. Insert the wire end into the cones. Hot-glue the edge of the wire to the jute.

Sweet Music Trim

Tiny strips of sheet music rolled inside a clear glass ball set the tone for your holiday tree.

WHAT YOU NEED

Purchased clear glass ornament with removable top • Old Christmas sheet music • Pencil • Scissors • Narrow ribbon

WHAT YOU DO

Be sure the ornament is clean and dry. Remove the top. Cut small strips of sheet music and coil around the pencil. Remove from pencil and place inside the ornament. Put top back on ornament. Add ribbon for hanging.

Add a bit of sparkle and shine to your holiday decorating with glistening ornaments displayed in clear glass vessels.

Bejeweled Ornament

Combine sparkling jewels in silver and a gold globe ball to make a stunning ornament for your holiday tree.

WHAT YOU NEED
Purchased matte-finish gold ornament • Jewels in desired shapes • Crafts glue • Gold ribbon

WHAT YOU DO
Be sure the ornament is clean and dry. Plan your design first. Here, the jewels are grouped at the top and cascade down the sides of the ornament. Glue in place. Let dry. Add a ribbon for hanging.

Sparkling Goblets

For a quick centerpiece or table favor that is sure to shine, fill clear glass goblets with small vintage ornaments and, if desired, a sprig of evergreen. Group the goblets together for a stunning centerpiece.

The Wish List

You want your gifts to be perfect for everyone on your Christmas list! Take time to make a special handmade gift presented in a beautifully wrapped box and you are sure to please!

Pretty Gift Soaps

A purchased bar of soap can become an elegant gift when you add your own pretty label or tag and a snippet of ribbon.

WHAT YOU NEED

Large purchased bars of soap • Patterned paper • Cardstock • Coordinating ribbon • Small hole punch • Computer/printer or stamps • Twine or cording • Scissors • Adhesive, including strong double-sided tape and foam dots

WHAT YOU DO

1. Remove any printed wrappers from soap. Leave clear wrappers in place.

2. Cut two wide strips of paper to wrap around the soap, one a bit narrower than the other. Adhere the strips together.

3. Bend and form the strips to fit around the soap, adhering the strips to the plastic wrapper. Adhere the cut ends with heavy double-sided tape at the bottom of the soap.

4. To make a tag, print or stamp the name of the soap onto decorative paper or cardstock, mat on cardstock, punch a small hole, and string it onto twine or cording.

5. Wrap ribbon around the soap; tie in a bow on top. Tie the tag to the ribbon, slipping it under the bow's knot.

6. To make a ribbon-laced label, print or stamp the name of the soap onto decorative paper or cardstock, then punch a small hole at each end of the label.

7. Thread ribbon through one hole, extending it along the underside of the label and out the other hole. Adhere the label to the top of the soap with foam dots.

8. Stretch the ribbon around the soap and adhere at the bottom with double-sided tape.

Stacked Up

For the coffee lover on your list, wrap some fresh coffee beans in Christmas-color espresso cups.

WHAT YOU NEED

Two expresso or other coffee cups • Fresh coffee beans • 1½-inch-wide ribbon • ¼-inch-wide ribbon • Vintage spoon • Cellophane • Rubber band • Gift tag

WHAT YOU DO

1. Fill coffee cups with fresh coffee beans and stack on top of each other. Cut the cellophane large enough to pull around the stacked cups. Pull around the cups and secure with the rubber band.

2. Tie a piece of narrow ribbon around the spoon and around the rubber band. Wrap the wider ribbon around the cups and tie at the top. Add a gift tag.

Origami Note Card Set

To make an elegant gift, layer beautiful origami papers on cardstock to make one-of-a-kind note cards. Then tuck them into a handmade box.

WHAT YOU NEED

Origami papers • Metallic paper • Cardstock for card bases and box • Matching A2 (invitation-size) envelopes • Die-cut flourishes • Circle punches or die cuts in two sizes • Adhesive, including strong tape adhesive and foam dots • Scoring board or blade • Optional: Printer or letter stamps for monograms • Mini brads • Piercing tool • Matching pen

WHAT YOU DO

For notecards

1. Cut cardstock to 5½×8½ inches for card bases. Score and fold card bases in half to create cards measuring 5½×4¼ inches. (A2 invitation size).

2. Cut a rectangle of smooth cardstock and adhere to inside of each card. Cut a rectangle of metallic paper and adhere to the front of each card. Cut origami paper to fit the fronts of cards as desired.

3. Copy text onto cardstock and cut out. Use a piercing tool to make holes, insert brads, then adhere to the card fronts with foam dots. Add die-cut flourishes cut from metallic paper to the fronts of the cards as desired.

4. To make monogram cards, print or stamp a letter or medallion, then punch with smallest size circle punch. Mat on contrasting cardstock punched from the larger size.

For box

1. Trim cardstock to 8×8 inches. Referring to diagram, below, score 1¼ inches from the left and right edges. Score 3¼ inches from the other two edges.

2. Cut slits as shown in diagram, below, then fold on score lines. Adhere sides of box with strong tape adhesive.

3. Score and adhere wide strips of metallic paper around the top portion of the box. Trim with origami paper and a matted monogram letter. Insert cards into box with envelopes on end at back. Place pen in box.

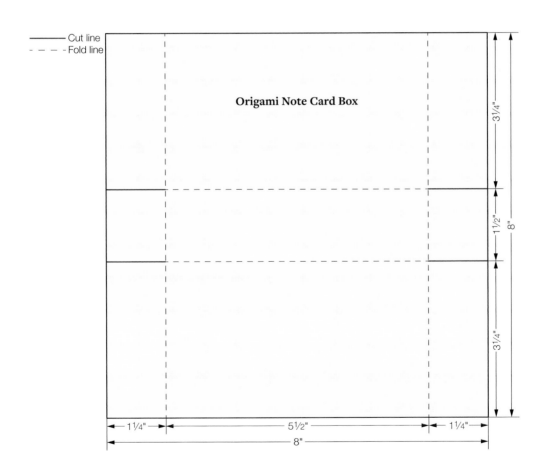

Chalk-Top Containers

Fill jars with holiday treats and then mark the tops with a chalk label for a perfect little gift.

WHAT YOU NEED
Small glass jars with flat lids such as canning or jelly jars • Blackboard paint • Paintbrush • White chalk

WHAT YOU DO
Remove the lids from the jars and paint with chalkboard paint. Let dry. Use white chalk to write the contents of the jar on the jar lid. Place the treats in the jar and put lids on jars.

Button Magnets

Bright-colored buttons and some narrow ribbon combine with purchased magnet backs to make a quick and useful gift.

WHAT YOU NEED
Large, flat 2-hole buttons • Narrow ribbon • Flat round magnet (available at crafts stores) • Crafts glue

WHAT YOU DO
Thread the ribbon through the holes of the buttons starting from the back side. Turn button over and glue the magnet to the back. Let dry.

Felted Sweater Bag

Don't throw that cozy wool old sweater away! Instead, make a stylish purse that is sure to be treasured.

WHAT YOU NEED

Tracing paper • Pencil • Preshrunk felted sweater • 64 inches of ⅜-inch cording, cut into two 32-inch lengths • ½ yard of ¼-inch cording, cut into two 9-inch lengths • ¼ yard heavyweight iron-on interfacing • ¼ yard lining fabric • Matching thread • Scissors

WHAT YOU DO

1. Enlarge and trace purse patterns, below, and cut out. Cut purse pieces from sweater bottom, aligning top straight edge of pattern with the bottom of the sweater so that the ribbing extends beyond the straight edge. Cut handles from straight grain of remaining sweater fabric, piecing if needed to make two strips 1½×32 inches long and two strips ¾×8 inches long. Cut pocket from sweater front or make one from sweater fabric, using pocket pattern piece.

2. Iron interfacing to wrong sides of purse sweater fabric. With right sides together, sew side and lower edges of purse, starting and stopping on side edges at the point where the sweater ribbing beings. Use a ¼-inch seam allowance. Clip curves and turn right side out.

3. With wrong sides together, sew remaining side edges of ribbing on purse. Fold ribbing edge to outside of purse. Edgestitch pocket piece to the center of one right side of lining piece, about 1½ inches from top straight edge. With wrong sides together, stitch side and lower edges of lining pieces together using ¼-inch seam. Fold top edge of lining ½ inch to wrong side and iron flat. Fold each ¾×8-inch strip of fabric around the ¼-inch cording.

4. Using matching thread, hand-stitch long cut edges together around cording. Fold one wrapped cord in half to make a loop and baste in place at center top of back of purse, extending cut edges ¾ inch into purse from top fold edge of ribbing. With other wrapped narrow cord, tie a loose knot in center as a clasp. Fold in half and baste in place at opposite top edge of purse.

5. Wrap each 32-inch length of ⅜-inch cording with sweater fabric and hand-sew long cut edges and each short end of strips. On outside of purse front and back, make small holes to insert handles by clipping slits ¼ inch wide and ⅜ inch long at points marked on pattern, making sure this spot is just under the sweater cuff folded over. Tack the clipped pieces to the backside by taking a few hand stitches.

6. Tie loose knot in one end of each handle. Insert long straight end of each handle through a hole from the front side of purse, then from back side to the outside on the remaining hole. Tie another loose knot near end of handle. Insert other handle through purse in the same manner.

7. Pin handles to purse at top edges and baste in place at top folded edge, keeping ribbing free. Put lining inside purse, with wrong side of lining facing wrong side of purse. Edgestitch around top edge at fold line, through handles, loop, and knot clasp, laying ribbing out flat. Fold ribbing down to outside of purse to finish.

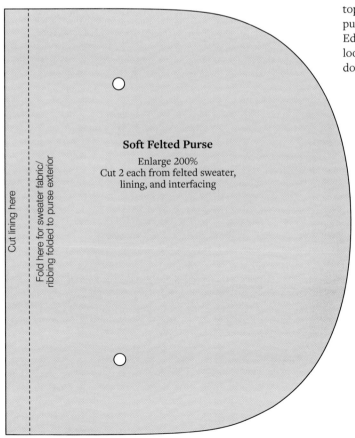

Soft Felted Purse
Enlarge 200%
Cut 2 each from felted sweater, lining, and interfacing

Cut lining here

Fold here for sweater fabric/ ribbing folded to purse exterior

Soft Felted Purse Inside Pocket
Enlarge 200%
Cut 1 felted sweater or lining fabric

Blooming Flower Pins and Headbands

Add a touch of whimsy and color to winter wardrobes. Vintage buttons make eye-catching flower centers for the pins and the headbands. Stitch up a whole bouquet—they make wonderful gifts for teachers, friends, and neighbors.

WHAT YOU NEED

Wool felt such as National Nonwovens in red, blush, cherry red, beige, and white • ½-inch and ¾-inch vintage buttons • ½-inch pin back or headband • Scraps of green silk in light green • Scraps of white and off-white woven wool • Off-white thread • Die cut tool such as Sizzix Big Kick die cut machine • 1 to 3½-inch flower dies • Sewing machine • Sewing needle

WHAT YOU DO

For the Brooches

1. Note: There are many different ways to assemble petals for the brooches. You can purchase cut felt flowers in the button section of fabric stores, salvage silk petals from artificial flowers, or use a die-cutting machine to cut flowers out of felt. We used a die-cutting machine for the brooches, and we used the patterns, below, for the flower headband.

2. Use the pattern, below, as your guide to cut a silk leaf and a woven wool leaf. Stack one over the other and pin them together. Machine stitch around the outside edge and then make a center seam up the middle.

3. Stack the flowers together, arranging them largest to smallest. Position a button in the center of the flower. A small change of color or button makes a big change to the flower. Find the combination you like best.

4. Bring your needle and thread up through the layers of felt petals. Hook the needle through the buttons before going back down through the flower petals. Once you reach the base of the flowers, repeat the stitch two or three more times to ensure the petals and buttons are firmly connected.

5. While the thread is still attached, stitch a leaf and pin back to the underside of the flowers. Make several more stitches to strengthen the connection, then hide your knot between the flower petals.

For the White Rosette Headband or Dark Pink Headband

1. Cut out two 4-inch-diameter circles and one 3-inch-diameter circle. Using fabric scissors on the felt circles, cut wavy line all around. Then cut a wavy spiral line around until you reach the center.

2. Starting in the center, coil the cut piece around to form a rosette. Hot-glue to secure. Finish flowers by gluing a red bead or button to the center. Trace the leaf patterns, below, and cut out from green felt if desired. Glue one or three rosettes and leaves onto headband.

For the Fuchsia Flower Headband

1. Trace patterns, below. Cut two flower shapes from fuschia or pink felt, one smaller than the other. Stack together.

2. Push a decorative brad down through both layers to secure. Hot-glue to headband.

Headband Flower
Full-Size Pattern
Cut 1

Leaf
Full-Size Pattern
Cut 1

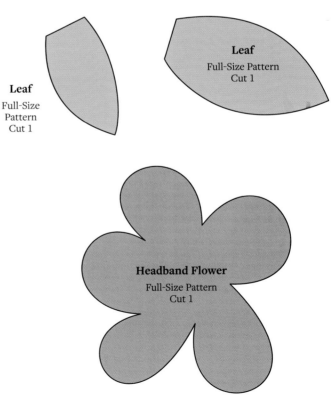

Leaf
Full-Size Pattern
Cut 1

Headband Flower
Full-Size Pattern
Cut 1

Checked Baby Hat

Keep his little head warm with a sweet hat made from a recycled sweater and little-boy checked fabric.

WHAT YOU NEED
Tracing paper • Pencil • ¼ yard of blue-and-white checked fabric • ½ yard of lining fabric • Felted sweater fabric from recycled sweater including ribbed edge • Scissors • Matching sewing thread • Small piece of hook and loop fastener such as Velcro

WHAT YOU DO
1. Enlarge and trace pattern pieces, opposite, and cut out. In addition, cut a 5×11½- inch piece of checked fabric and lining for the top center panel. Trace around patterns onto fabrics and cut out using the ribbed edge of felted sweater for the inside bill of hat.
2. With right sides together, stitch hat lining sides to center panel lining section together with right sides together. Stitch hat felted sweater pieces together wrong sides together so seams are exposed. Or stitch with right sides together if you prefer to have no exposed seams.
3. To make ear flaps and bill, stitch lining to felted sweater fabric, right sides together. Clip curves as needed. Turn and press flat.
4. Pin bill of hat to front raw edge of cap, matching centers. Pin ear flap to back of hat, matching center backs. Baste. Pin lining to hat, right sides together. Stitch all layers together, leaving an opening for turning. Turn and whip stitch opening closed.
5. Cut two pieces of checked fabric 5×3 inches long for straps. Fold and press to hide raw edges. Tack to ear flaps. Add hook and loop fastener to ends.

Ribboned Baby Cloths

Every new mother or grandmother would love to have a set of these colorful and very useful baby cloths to use after baby's feeding. Choose ribbons that match the colors of the nursery or baby's favorite color.

WHAT YOU NEED
Purchased cloth baby diapers with double-thickness center • Cotton ribbon in desired colors and patterns • Sewing machine

WHAT YOU DO
Wash and dry the diapers. Press. Lay the ribbon vertically on the diaper and machine-zigzag in rows on the diaper. Press, fold, and stack. Place in box for gift.

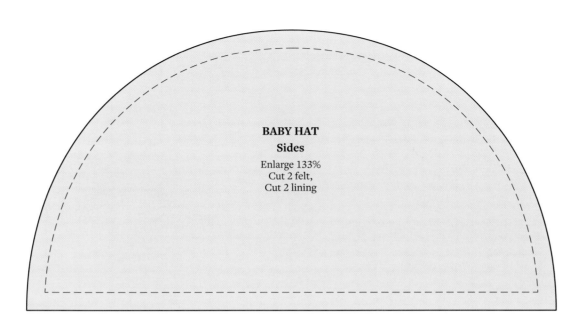

BABY HAT

Sides

Enlarge 133%
Cut 2 felt,
Cut 2 lining

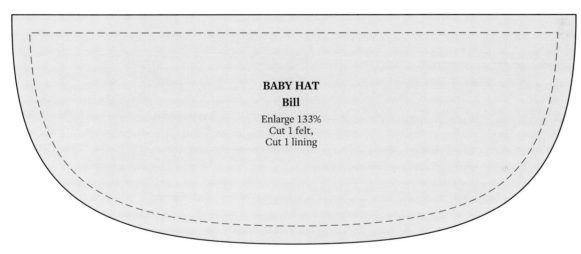

BABY HAT

Bill

Enlarge 133%
Cut 1 felt,
Cut 1 lining

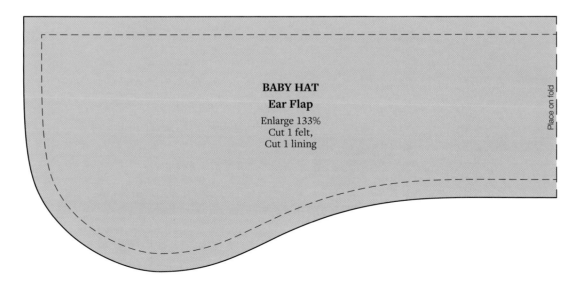

BABY HAT

Ear Flap

Enlarge 133%
Cut 1 felt,
Cut 1 lining

Place on fold

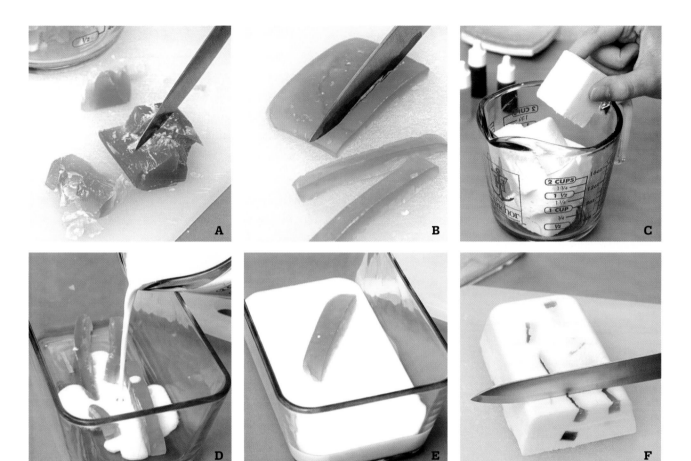

Homemade Art Soaps

You'll feel like a sculptor as you create these beautiful and smooth pieces of art. Slice them to see the glorious creations you have made!

WHAT YOU NEED

Blocks of transparent glycerine soap in desired colors • Blocks of coconut or opaque soap in desired colors • Flat pan • Sharp knife • Glass measuring cups • Microwave • Nonstick cooking spray • Bread pan or desired pan • Soap coloring and fragrance (optional)

WHAT YOU DO

1. Spray both the flat pan and bread pan with nonstick cooking spray. Set aside.
2. Cut the pieces of the transparent soap into small chunks and place in glass measuring cup. See Photo A. Microwave until just melted. Pour into flat pan until about ¾ inch thick. Let set until hard.
3. Lay the cooled transparent soap slab on a cutting board and cut into long pieces. See Photo B. Place the pieces in the bottom of the bread pan. Set aside.
4. Cube and place the opaque soap pieces in another measuring cup. See Photo C. Add coloring and fragrance if desired. Microwave until just melted. Pour over the transparent strips in the pan until just covered. See Photo D. Let set until a thin skin forms on top of the warm soap. This will take only a few minutes.
5. Add another layer of the transparent soap strips, carefully laying them on the opaque soap. See Photo E. Pour more of the opaque soap on the top. Continue adding layers if desired. Let soap cool completely.
6. Lay cooled soap on a cutting board and slice with a large knife. See Photo F.
7. Wrap soaps in cellophane or package as desired.

Mini Mitten

So lively and quick to knit, this tiny mitten offers a triple Christmas treat. Tie one to a package and it's a bright decoration. Slip a gift card, a name card, or a cash gift inside and it becomes an envelope. Make them by the handfuls and they're trims for the tree.

WHAT YOU NEED
Red Heart Classic (Art. E267) 100 percent acrylic worsted-weight yarn: one skein of Cherry Red #0319 • Size 8 (5mm) knitting needles • Stitch holder or large safety pin • Two place markers or yarn scrap of another color • Two snowflake-shape buttons

WHAT YOU DO
With mc and leaving a 6-inch tail for a hanging loop, cast on 23 sts.

Row 1 (RS): *K1, p 1; rep from * across.

Row 2 (WS): *P 1, k 1; rep from * across.

Row 3: Rep Row 1.

Row 4: P across.

Row 5: K across.

Row 6: P across.

Row 7: K 11, pm, M1, k 1, M1, pm, k 11—25 sts.

Row 8: P across.

Row 9: K to marker, sl marker, M1, k to marker, M1, sl marker, k to end of row.

Rows 10–13: Rep rows 8 and 9 until there are 9 sts between markers—31 sts.

Row 14: P across (remove markers).

Row 15 (RS): K 11, place next 9 sts on holder (this will be the thumb), k 11.

Rows 16–20: Rep (rows 4 and 5) twice; rep Row 4.

Top Shaping
Row 21 (RS): Ssk, k 7, k2tog, ssk, k 7, k2tog.

Row 22: P across.

Row 23: Ssk, k 5, k2tog, ssk, k 5, k2tog.

Row 24: P across.

Row 25: K2tog to the end—7 sts. Cut yarn, leaving a long tail.

Starting at last st on needle, thread tail through 7 sts remaining, going around twice. Pull tight to close top opening. Sew sides together (WS out).

Thumb
Turn mitten RS out. Return sts to needle. Starting on WS, p 9 sts. On RS, k 1, k2tog to the end—5 sts. Cut yarn, leaving a 6-inch tail. Close thumb as for Top Shaping. Weave loose end into WS of work.

Finishing
Sew snowflake buttons to mitten front. Create hanging loop, weaving loose end of beg tail to opposite side on WS of mitten cuff.

KNIT ABBREVIATIONS	
k	knit
k2tog	knit 2 stitches together
M1	make 1 stitch
mc	main color
p	purl
pm	place marker
rep	repeat
RS	right side
sl	slip
ssk	slip, slip, knit (slip 2 stitches, 1 at a time knitwise, insert left needle and knit 2 together)
st(s)	stitch(es)
WS	wrong side
*	repeat instructions following * as directed

Child's Poinsettia Purse

Any little girl would love to carry her own special bag at Christmastime. Fill it with tiny books or some other sweet surprises.

WHAT YOU NEED

Tracing paper • Pencil • Scissors • Two 12×12-inch squares of red felt • One 12×12-inch square of lime green felt • Scrap of light yellow felt • Fabric glue • Lime green cording • Matching sewing thread • Needle • ½ yard of red rickrack • 9 lime green beads • Green and red embroidery thread • Large button

WHAT YOU DO

1. Trace patterns, opposite, and cut out. Copy onto felt pieces and cut out. Lay green leaves in place behind flower front and adhere with fabric glue. Adhere gold circle to front with fabric glue. With needle and thread, tack cording around circle in scallop pattern. Sew a bead where cording meets the circle edge.

2. Pin flower back to flower front wrong sides together. Stitch around edges, leaving top open. Embroider veins on leaves using chain stitch.

3. Thread button with small piece of red embroidery floss. Tie a knot on button front. Glue button to purse front. Tack rickrack at opening corners for handle.

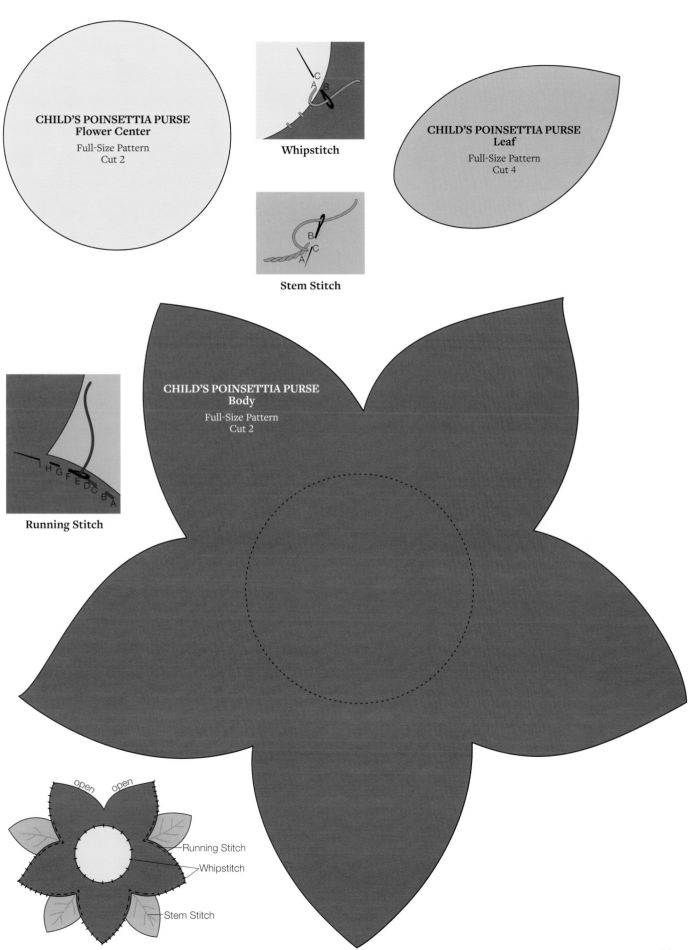

CHILD'S POINSETTIA PURSE
Flower Center
Full-Size Pattern
Cut 2

Whipstitch

CHILD'S POINSETTIA PURSE
Leaf
Full-Size Pattern
Cut 4

Stem Stitch

CHILD'S POINSETTIA PURSE
Body
Full-Size Pattern
Cut 2

Running Stitch

open   open

Running Stitch

Whipstitch

Stem Stitch

Pretty Packages and Gift Tags

Make your gift giving even more special by embellishing your gift boxes with holiday motifs you create yourself. Then add a personalized gift tag that will complete your gift.

WHAT YOU NEED

Gift boxes with lids • Patterned scrapbook paper in a variety of coordinated colors/designs • Matching cardstock • Border punch • Scissors • Circle cutter and scalloped circle die cuts/punches • Scalloped die cut • Seasonal die cuts or punches • Sticker or stamps for creating monograms • Scoring tool • Twine or cording • Decorative ribbon • Adhesive, including strong tape adhesive, foam dots, glue dots, and fine-tip liquid adhesive • Pearlescent craft paint, such as Liquid Pearls • Short length of jewelry-making wire • Large and small manila tags

WHAT YOU DO

For for small wrapped package (snowflake on top):
1. Measure box and cut paper to fit sides, lid, and lid edges. Apply strong tape adhesive to the back side of the paper and adhere to the box and lid.
2. Place gift in box, then tape strips of patterned paper to the bottom of the box, up each side, and to the top of the box.
3. Cut circles or use die-cut circles and scalloped circles for the top of the box adhering with foam dots. Adhere a decorative die-cut shape (snowflake) to the top of the box using foam dots.
4. Stamp or use a sticker for the monogram letter on a circle. Mat on a scalloped circle and adhere to one of the banner strips.

For the for large wrapped package (ornaments on side):

1. Trace patterns, below, onto tracing paper. Set aside. Measure box and cut paper to fit sides, lid, and lid edges. Apply strong tape adhesive to the back side of the paper and adhere to the box and lid.
2. Print or stamp a large monogram letter on a cardstock or paper circle, mat, and adhere to the top of the box using foam dots. Trace the ornament patterns onto the back sides of patterned paper.
3. Tape twine or cording to the inside of the box and extend the other end to the spots where the ornaments will be adhered; tape twine in place. Cut out and adhere ornaments to the side of the box using foam dots, covering the end of the twine or cording. Embellish as desired.

Instructions for Small Snowflake Tag (page 103):

1. Cover the top and bottom portion of the small manila tag with cardstock and patterned paper. Punch a border from cardstock and adhere horizontally to the center of the tag. Cut a strip of striped paper and adhere, overlapping the border.
2. Wrap twine or cording around the tag and tie in a bow at the right. Secure with a dot of liquid glue. Adhere a small circle to the top of the tag and punch a hole for ribbon. Die- cut or punch a snowflake from cardstock; emboss and adhere to a die-cut circle. Mat on a scalloped circle using foam dots.
3. Copy tag text onto cardstock and cut out, notching ends to create a banner. Adhere to the bottom of the tag. Tie tag to package using decorative ribbon.

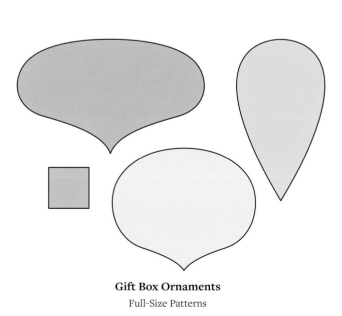

Gift Box Ornaments
Full-Size Patterns

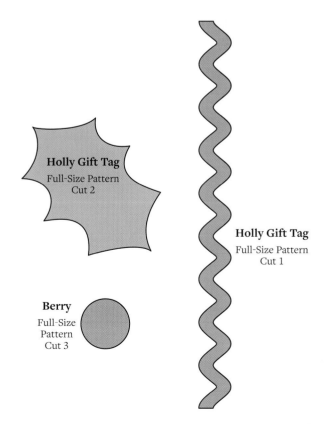

Holly Gift Tag
Full-Size Pattern
Cut 2

Holly Gift Tag
Full-Size Pattern
Cut 1

Berry
Full-Size
Pattern
Cut 3

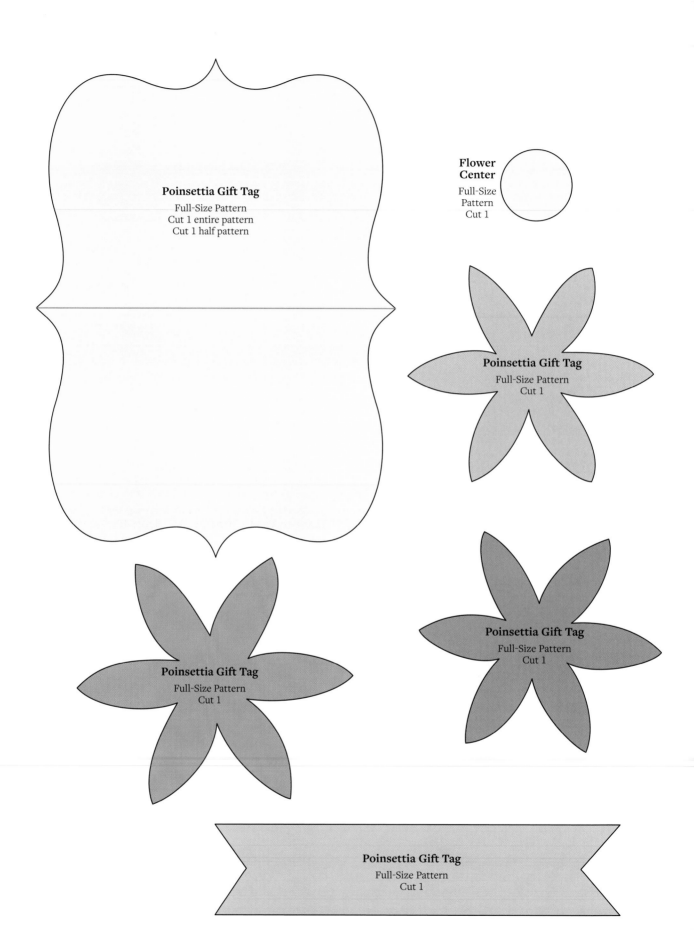

Poinsettia Gift Tag

Full-Size Pattern
Cut 1 entire pattern
Cut 1 half pattern

Flower Center
Full-Size
Pattern
Cut 1

Poinsettia Gift Tag

Full-Size Pattern
Cut 1

Poinsettia Gift Tag

Full-Size Pattern
Cut 1

Poinsettia Gift Tag

Full-Size Pattern
Cut 1

Poinsettia Gift Tag

Full-Size Pattern
Cut 1

SMALL
SNOWFLAKE
TAG

POINSETTIA
TAG

HOLLY
GIFT TAG

LARGE
SNOWFLAKE
ORNAMENT TAG

Instructions for Poinsettia Tag:

1. Trace patterns, opposite, onto tracing paper and cut out. Set aside. Cut scalloped shape from cardstock, then cover the bottom portion with patterned paper. Adhere a small punched circle to the top of the tag, then punch a hole through it. Cut notched ribbon pattern from patterned paper and adhere horizontally across tag.

2. Trace poinsettia flowers onto back side of patterned paper; cut out. Emboss flowers if desired. Adhere the poinsettia to the center of the tag using foam dots. Copy the tag text onto cardstock and cut out. Adhere to tag, tucking top under the flower. Tie tag to package using decorative ribbon.

Instructions for Large Snowflake Ornament Tag:

1. Cover the large manila tag with patterned paper or cardstock. Adhere a small punched circle to the top of the tag, then punch a hole through it. Copy text onto cardstock and cut out; adhere to bottom of tag.

2. Die-cut or cut a large snowflake from cardstock and patterned paper. Adhere to the tag, extending off side. Add layers of paper and a punched or die-cut shape to the ornament for trim. Tie the tag to the package using decorative ribbon.

Instructions for Holly Gift Tag:

1. Trace patterns, page 101, and cut out. Set aside. Cut a 3½-inch circle from cardstock to create ornament base. Cut a 3-inch circle from patterned paper and adhere to the cardstock base.

2. To create ornament top, cut a 1¼×2½-inch strip of cardstock and fold in half. Make a loop from jewelry wire and place inside cardstock strip, then tape to the back side of the ornament.

3. Copy text onto light-color cardstock and adhere to lower portion of ornament; trim. Cut zigzag border from colored cardstock and adhere just below text.

4. Trace holly leaves onto cardstock and cut out; score down the center of each leaf and emboss and adhere to top portion of ornament. Cut three red berries and adhere atop leaves. Tie a small bow from twine and adhere to the top of the ornament. Tie a second bow from ribbon and adhere over the top of the twine. Attach tag to package using wire loop.

Festive Felt

Cue the elves. It's time to set the scene with
fanciful felt poinsettias, stockings, ornaments,
and more. Rich in color and texture, this
soft but very forgivable fabric is soon
to be your best crafting friend.

Heart Ornaments

Scandinavian design has never been easier to create at home. Simply stack and stitch felt strips, then cut them apart into piles of hearts. Leave the hearts as singles or glue them together into multilayered hearts or snowflakes. They make cheery gift toppers or ornaments. Don't put them away at the end of the holidays; they're perfect for Valentine's Day too.

WHAT YOU NEED
Red felt, preferably with 30% wool content such as Woolfelt National Nonwovens • Red thread • Natural twine/hemp cord • 9-mm unfinished wood beads • Hot-glue gun and glue sticks • Rotary cutter, straight edge, and cutting mat • Sewing machine • Scissors

WHAT YOU DO

For the Heart Shape:
1. Using the mat, straight edge, and rotary cutter, cut the felt into uniform strips. Maximize the available length to yield the most hearts per strip. The width of the strip dictates the size of the hearts; 1½-inch strips will make small 1-inch hearts, 2½-inch strips will make medium 2-inch hearts, 3½-inch strips will make large 3-inch hearts. The higher the wool content the thicker and stronger the hearts. **Note:** We used four strips for each heart, two strips on each side. If you're using higher than 30% wool content, you can forgo the doubling; a single layer will be sturdy enough.
2. Stack four strips of the same length and width together. Machine stitch along the top edge. Position your seam as close as possible to the edge while still catching all four layers of felt.
3. Divide the strips in half. Bring both sides down below the first seam; you should see the heart take shape on either end of the strip. Pin the length of the strip together and make a second seam along the bottom edge, trapping all four layers.

4. Cut ¼- to ½-inch-thick hearts off the strip. Pick a width and cut all the hearts the same thickness so that you can assemble them into snowflakes, heartstrings, or multilayered hearts. Assemble the hearts into flowing shapes and hot-glue in place.

To Make Hearts into Snowflakes:
1. Select six hearts that are the same size. Glue the first two together. Add a drop of glue to the base of the heart and another drop of glue to the widest point of the curved top.
2. Repeat the process to add a third heart; pinch the insides of the hearts together while the outsides are gluing together. Continue adding the three remaining hearts. The last heart will glue to the first heart.

For the Heart Strings:
1. Select three different-size hearts. Glue the base of the smallest heart down into the center top of the medium heart. Then glue the base of the medium heart down into the center top of the largest heart.
2. Apply pressure to the glued areas together for a minute until the glue sets.

For the Multilayer Single Heart:
1. Select a large and small heart. Glue the base of the small heart to the inside of the base of the large heart. Then apply glue to the inside center seam of the large heart, gluing it to the top of the small heart.

To Finish All Shapes:
Cut the twine into 5-inch lengths, one for each finished shape. Fold the length in half; tie the ends together into an overhand knot. String a bead up onto the folded end so it rests under the knot. Hot-glue the folded end into the center top of the heart; pinch the felt around the twine while the glue sets.

Flower Garland

A simple strand of felt flowers instantly adds homespun charm to your mantel or tree. Cut the flower shapes from patterns or use a die-cutting machine. Die-cutting machines and hot glue speed the assembly process, allowing you to create a lengthy garland in record time.

WHAT YOU NEED
Tracing paper • Pencil • Wool felt such as National Nonwovens wool felt in desired colors • Embroidery floss • Sewing thread • ¼-inch variegated gray and white ribbon • Flower dies such as Sizzix Big Kick (optional) • Scissors • Embroidery floss and needle • Small buttons • Hot-glue gun and glue sticks

WHAT YOU DO
1. To make the flowers, trace patterns, right, onto tracing paper and cut out. Or make your own patterns. Trace around pattern onto desired colors of felt and cut out. Or use a die-cutting machine. You will need about 48 flowers cut from the felt colors for a garland. Each flower in the garland features three large flowers, two small flowers, two medium circles (2-inch, 1¾-inch), and two small circles (1¼-inch, 1-inch).

2. Arrange the felt flowers into stacked pairs. The garland is two-sided; each flower has two fronts that sandwich the ribbon. Stack the felt elements together largest to smallest, mixing colors and petal shapes, then top each stack with a button.

3. Sew the button to the center of each stack. Thread an embroidery needle with a full strand of floss, bring the needle up through the layers of petals, and stitch the button to the felt.

4. Glue the pairs of felt flowers to the ribbon. Spread the sewn pairs across your work surface. Alternate the colors and sizes so that the garland will be variegated and interesting. Hot-glue the backs of the pairs together, trapping the ribbon in between positioning the flowers about 3 inches apart. Let glue dry.

Just as pretty as blooms in a garden, felt flower pieces combine to make a lovely assortment of layered flowers to adorn your holiday tree.

Flower Garland
Full-Size Patterns

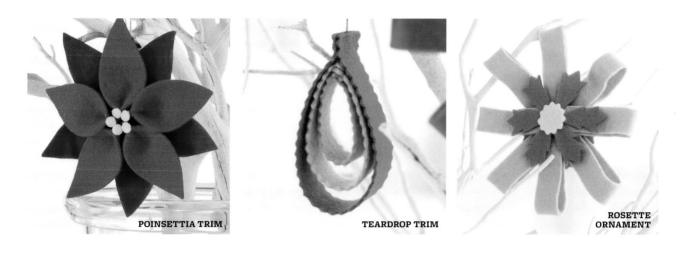

POINSETTIA TRIM

TEARDROP TRIM

ROSETTE ORNAMENT

Out on a Limb

Flex your tree-trimming skills by dangling colorful ornaments in varying styles on snow-white branches. Choose the ones you like or make the entire collection. They are so quick to make, you can make them all in the wink of an eye.

Poinsettia Trim

WHAT YOU NEED

Tracing paper • Lightweight cardboard • Freezer paper • Wool felt (white, dark red, and red) • Iron • Fabric glue • Clip clothespins • Hole punch • Removable double-sided tape

WHAT YOU DO

1. Trace patterns, pages 112–113, onto tracing paper; cut out. Trace patterns onto lightweight cardboard; cut out.
2. Using an iron on medium heat, press freezer paper, shiny side down, onto felt. Trace patterns on the freezer paper. Trace small poinsettia onto dark red felt and small leaf onto red felt the number of times indicated on patterns. Cut out shapes and peel off freezer paper.
3. Dab fabric glue on right side of one inside corner of petal; pinch together, holding in place with a clothespin. Repeat for each leaf. Let glue dry; remove clothespins. Apply fabric glue to back of leaf; glue to poinsettia between petals. Repeat with other leaves. Use a hole punch to create five dots from white felt. Glue a dot over glued seam of each folded petal.

Teardrop Trim

WHAT YOU NEED

Pinking shears • Wool felt in three colors • Fabric glue • String

WHAT YOU DO

1. Using pinking shears, cut felt into ½-inch-wide strips in the following lengths: 5, 6, and 8½ inches. Form the 5-inch-long strip into a circle, slightly overlapping the ends; glue to secure. Loop the 6-inch-long strip around the 5-inch circle; glue to secure.
2. Referring to the photo, above, wrap the last felt strip around the smaller two loops, adding a hanging loop of string between the large loop ends; glue together to secure.

Rosette Ornament

WHAT YOU NEED

Wool felt in desired colors • Fabric glue • String

WHAT YOU DO

1. Cut four 1×9-inch strips from the desired color of felt. Fold in short ends to the center of one strip and glue in place, forming a double-petal loop.
2. Repeat with a second felt strip. Glue double-petal loop. Repeat with a second felt strip. Glue double-petal loops together in an X shape. Repeat with remaining two strips.
3. To form a rosette, glue together X shapes, setting loops of one X between loops of the other. Glue a felt embellishment, such as a snowflake or circle, on both sides in center of rosette. Thread string through one felt loop and knot ends to create a hanging loop.

continued on next page

TREE CUTOUT

SNOWFLAKE ORNAMENT

FELT DROP ORNAMENT

continued from previous page

Tree Cutout

WHAT YOU NEED

Tracing paper • Freezer paper • Wool felt (red, light green, green, brown, and aqua) • Iron • Pinking shears • Fabric glue • Baker's twine

WHAT YOU DO

1. Trace pattern, below, onto tracing paper and cut out. Using an iron on medium heat, adhere freezer paper, shiny side down, to each color of felt.
2. Referring to photo, above, trace pattern shapes on respective felt colors. Cut out shapes, using pinking shears to cut bottom edge of each tree branch. Peel off freezer paper. Glue tree shapes to red oval.
3. Glue a hanging loop of baker's twine to back of the red oval. Glue ornament to aqua felt, enclosing ends of hanging loop, and cut around shape using pinking shears.

Snowflake Ornament

WHAT YOU NEED

Tracing paper • Wool felt (orange, aqua, and white) • Fabric glue • Baker's twine • Pinking shears

WHAT YOU DO

1. Trace patterns from page 113 onto tracing paper and cut out. Cut one circle each from orange and aqua felt. Cut the snowflake pattern from the aqua circle, folding the shape in half to make the first series of cuts and then refolding in the opposite direction to make a second set of cuts.
2. Fold the shape in half on the diagonal to make a third set of cuts and then refold on the opposite diagonal to make a final set of cuts.

Felt Drop Ornaments

WHAT YOU NEED

Tracing paper • 1½×5-inch piece of paper • Quick-setting gel glue • 9×12-inch piece each of wool felt in two colors • Freezer paper • Iron • String • Two clear ¼-inch-diameter beads

WHAT YOU DO

1. Trace desired pattern, page 113, onto tracing paper and cut out. Roll the 1½×5-inch piece of paper into a ¼-inch-diameter cylinder that measures 5 inches long; secure with glue. **Note:** Trim ½ inch from length of the rolled paper for the shorter ornament. Cover cylinder with a layer of felt and glue in place.
2. Using an iron on medium heat, adhere freezer paper, shiny side down, to each color of felt. Using pattern, trace six shapes onto each color of felt. Cut out shapes. Peel off freezer paper.
3. Run a bead of quick-setting gel glue along the straight edge of each ornament piece and attach to the felt-covered cylinder, alternating colors, until all pieces are attached. Thread string through a small bead; tie ends in a knot to create a hanging loop. Glue bead inside the top of the cylinder. Glue remaining bead inside bottom of cylinder.

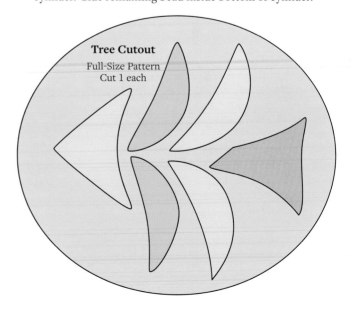

Tree Cutout
Full-Size Pattern
Cut 1 each

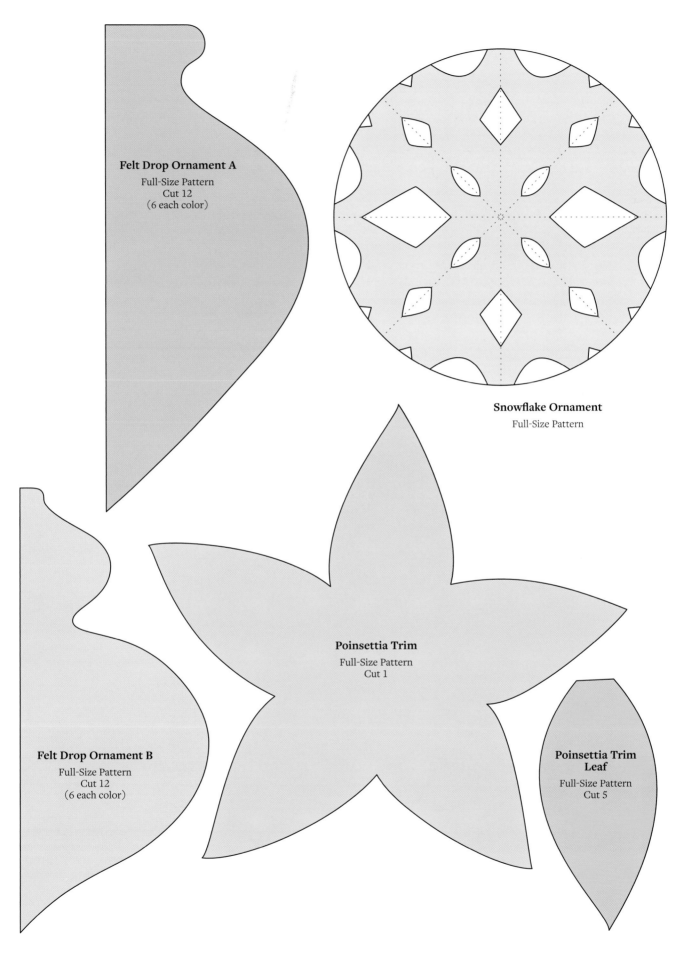

Felt Drop Ornament A

Full-Size Pattern
Cut 12
(6 each color)

Snowflake Ornament

Full-Size Pattern

Poinsettia Trim

Full-Size Pattern
Cut 1

Felt Drop Ornament B

Full-Size Pattern
Cut 12
(6 each color)

Poinsettia Trim Leaf

Full-Size Pattern
Cut 5

Felt Stocking Trio

Kick off the holidays by hanging stockings adorned with an exuberant mix of stripes, snowflakes, and circles. For the stockings trimmed with snowflakes, use clip art for the snowflake designs or draw your own using the photo as a guide.

Snowflakes Stocking

WHAT YOU NEED

Freezer paper • Iron • 18×24-inch rectangle of white wool felt • Scraps of wool felt (red, light blue, lime, and turquoise blue) • Quick-setting gel glue • ¾×46-inch strip of wool felt: turquoise blue • Pinking shears

WHAT YOU DO

1. Enlarge and trace (or use photo copier) stocking pattern, page 116, onto white paper; set aside.
2. Cut freezer paper into 5×7-inch sheets; flatten sheets under a stack of books. Print desired snowflake patterns onto dull sides of freezer-paper sheets. **Note:** We used snowflake designs from clipart.com and *414 Geometric Designs and Motifs* (Dover Publications). Separate the snowflakes.
3. Using the stocking pattern, cut a stocking front and a stocking back from white felt. Using a dry iron on medium heat, press freezer-paper snowflakes, shiny sides down, on desired colors of felt scraps. Cut out shapes and carefully peel off freezer paper.
4. Referring to the photo, opposite, arrange snowflakes on stocking front; adhere with quick-setting gel glue. Trim away excess parts of snowflakes. Glue the ¾×46-inch turquoise blue strip to wrong side of stocking front, starting and stopping at the top edge and letting strip extend about ⅜ inch beyond stocking edges as trim. Glue the stocking back to the stocking front, leaving open at the top.
5. Cut along the turquoise blue trim with pinking shears. From remaining white felt, cut a 1×10-inch strip for a hanging loop. Fold strip in half crosswise and glue ends inside stocking to stocking back, referring to photo, opposite, for placement.

Circles Stocking

WHAT YOU NEED

Tracing paper • Pencil • 18×24-inch rectangle of wool white felt • Freezer paper • Iron • Scraps of wool felt (red, light blue, lime, black, brown, green, royal blue, and turquoise blue) • Pinking shears • Quick-setting gel glue • ¾×46-inch strip of wool felt: turquoise blue

WHAT YOU DO

1. Enlarge and trace (or use photo copier) stocking pattern, page 116, onto white paper; set aside. Cut a stocking front and a stocking back from white felt.
2. Trace circle and starburst designs, page 116. Prepare the circle and starburst patterns and cut the felt following instructions for Snowflake Stocking, left.
Note: Cut out some circles using pinking shears. Peel off the freezer paper.
3. Referring to the photo, opposite, glue circles and starbursts to stocking front with quick-setting gel glue. Assemble and finish stocking as directed for Snowflakes Stocking, left.

Stripes Stocking

WHAT YOU NEED

Freezer paper • Iron • 18×24-inch rectangle of turquoise wool felt • Scraps of wool felt (lime, light blue, black, brown, white, and turquoise blue) • ¾×46-inch strip of white wool felt • Quick-setting gel glue • Pinking shears

WHAT YOU DO

1. Enlarge and trace (or use photo copier) stocking, heel, and toe patterns, page 116, onto white paper; set aside. Prepare the snowflake pattern, following instructions for the Snowflakes Stocking, left. **Note:** Print two snowflakes onto dull sides of freezer-paper sheets.
2. Using the patterns, cut a stocking front and a stocking back from turquoise blue felt and a heel and toe from lime felt. Referring to photo, opposite, cut felt scraps into various size strips to fit stocking front, trimming some with pinking shears. From brown felt, cut two ⅜×8-inch strips to outline inside edges of heel and toe. Using a dry iron on medium heat, press the freezer-paper snowflake shapes, shiny sides down, on light blue and turquoise blue felt. Cut out shapes and carefully peel off freezer paper. Cut light blue snowflake in half.
3. Referring to photo, opposite, arrange various size strips on stocking front and adhere with quick-setting gel glue. Glue turquoise blue snowflake and light blue snowflake halves on a wide white strip. Glue heel and toe shapes on stocking front. Adhere the ⅜×8-inch brown strips to inside edges of heel and toe and trim excess felt.
4. Assemble and finish stocking as directed for Snowflakes Stocking, using a ¾×46-inch white strip as trim and adding a turquoise blue hanging loop.

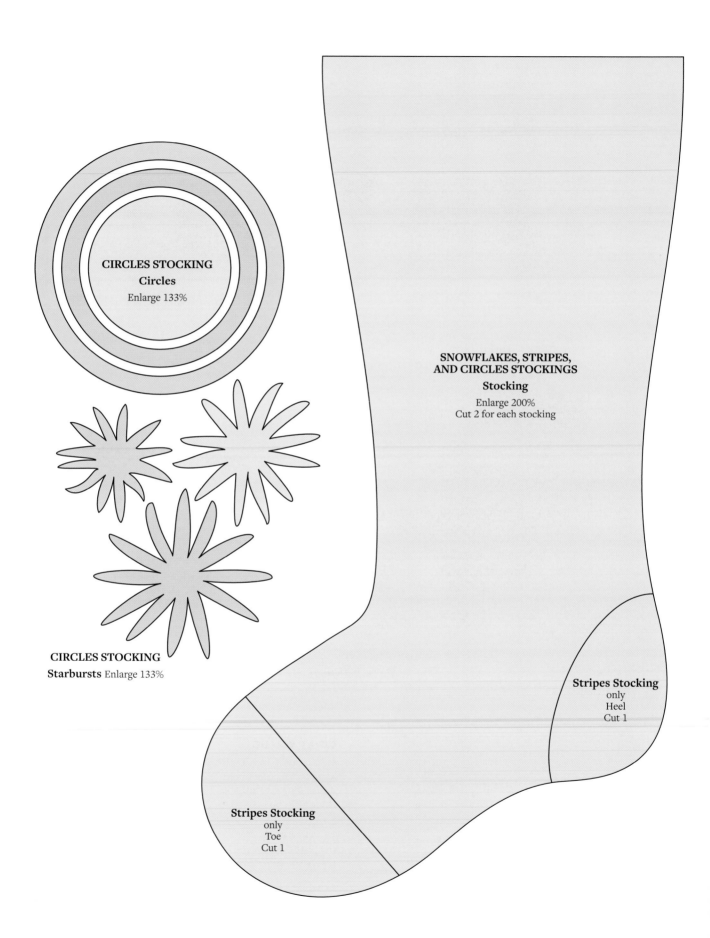

CIRCLES STOCKING
Circles
Enlarge 133%

**SNOWFLAKES, STRIPES,
AND CIRCLES STOCKINGS**
Stocking
Enlarge 200%
Cut 2 for each stocking

CIRCLES STOCKING
Starbursts Enlarge 133%

Stripes Stocking
only
Heel
Cut 1

Stripes Stocking
only
Toe
Cut 1

Striped Welcoming Wreath

A striped wreath that lasts from year to year lends a jolly vibe to interior doors. Nontraditional colors (see you later, red and green) give this wreath a modern spin.

WHAT YOU NEED
Felt Poinsettia Trim (see page 111) • Wool felt (turquoise blue, light blue, red, and lime) • Pinking shears • 12-inch-diameter foam beveled wreath • Straight pins

WHAT YOU DO
1. Follow the "Poinsettia Trim" instructions, page 111, to make a small red poinsettia. Set aside.
2. Use pinking shears to cut seven 2×8-inch strips each from turquoise blue, light blue, red, and lime felt using pinking shears. Referring to the photo, above, wrap strips around a foam wreath with each strip slightly overlapping the previous strip; pin strips to back of wreath. Pin felt poinsettia to wreath.

Star Bright

Your ornaments will sparkle when you add light-catching rhinestone and glass buttons to layered cutout felt stars.

WHAT YOU NEED

Tracing paper • Pencil • Scissors • Felt (dark blue, aqua, white, and dark red) • White embroidery floss • 1 rhinestone button • 5 small self-shank glass buttons • ¼-inch-wide white grosgrain ribbon • Fabric glue

WHAT YOU DO

1. Trace patterns, below, onto tracing paper. Cut out. Cut stars from dark blue, aqua, and white felt. Cut flower and circle shapes from different colors of felt. Set aside.

2. Embellish largest flower with French knots. Stitch rhinestone button to smallest blue circle. Then sew a small glass button to each star point. When all detailing is complete, stack the felt shapes, working from largest to smallest, and glue together with fabric glue.

3. Thread ribbon through the shank of one of the small glass buttons to hang the ornament.

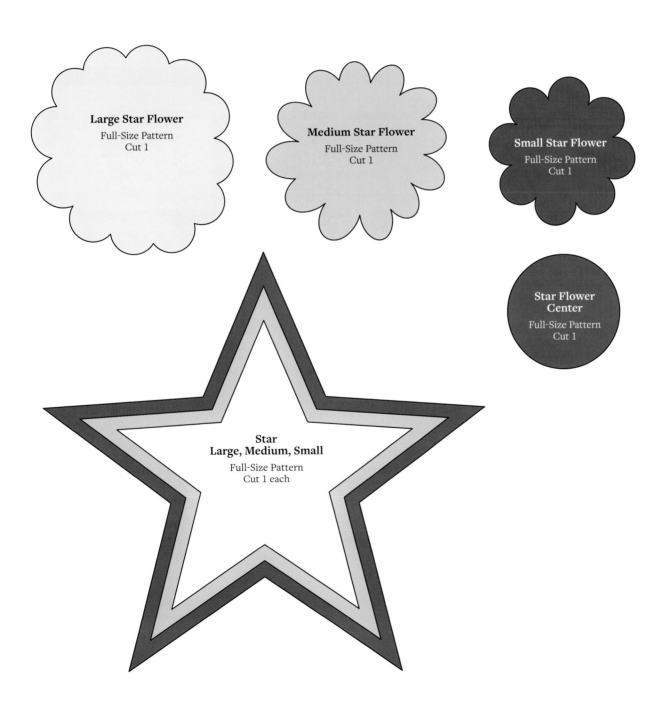

Large Star Flower
Full-Size Pattern
Cut 1

Medium Star Flower
Full-Size Pattern
Cut 1

Small Star Flower
Full-Size Pattern
Cut 1

Star Flower Center
Full-Size Pattern
Cut 1

Star
Large, Medium, Small
Full-Size Pattern
Cut 1 each

No need to go to a floral shop; create your own lovely poinsettia bloom using fun felt in bright holiday colors.

Heirloom Blooms

Using layered leaves of felt, create everlasting poinsettia stems that you can exhibit this season and for years to come. The pieces are layered and then stitched to create a three-dimensional effect.

WHAT YOU NEED

Tracing paper • Pencil • Scissors • Felt (bright red, dark red, dark blue, and aqua) • Green paper-covered floral wires • 6 round turquoise shank-style buttons • Blue and red embroidery floss

WHAT YOU DO

1. Trace patterns, opposite, onto tracing paper. For flower centers, cut six dark blue felt circles. Thread a floral wire through a felt circle and a button and twist the ends of the wire to secure. Repeat for all six buttons and circles; wire the stems together. Set aside.

2. Cut five small and seven larger leaf shapes each from bright red and dark red felt. Layer the bright red leaves atop the dark red leaves. Use a dark blue running stitch around the edges to secure. When stitching, leave an opening in the curved base of each leaf.

3. Make 2-inch loops at the ends of 12 floral wires. Insert a looped end into each petal base. Arrange small and then large petals around the button stem. Twist additional floral wires tightly around all of the stems to create one thick stem.

4. Cut five small petals each from dark blue and aqua felt. Stack the aqua felt on top of dark blue felt and secure with a centered red floss running stitch. Tuck the small petals under the buttons and adhere with fabric glue to the leaves.

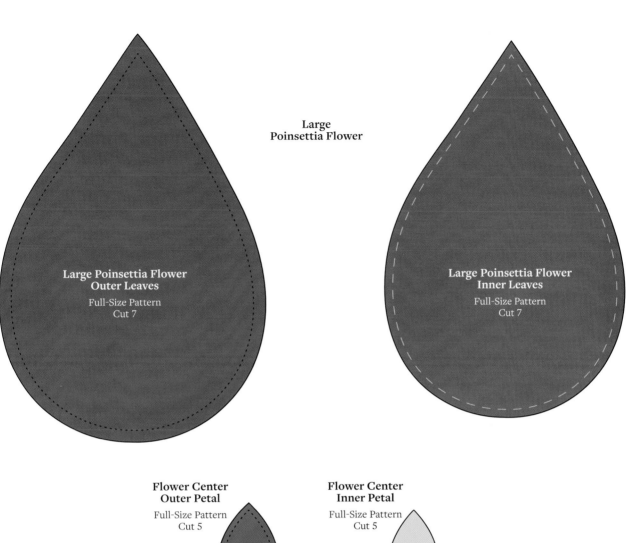

Large
Poinsettia Flower

**Large Poinsettia Flower
Outer Leaves**

Full-Size Pattern
Cut 7

**Large Poinsettia Flower
Inner Leaves**

Full-Size Pattern
Cut 7

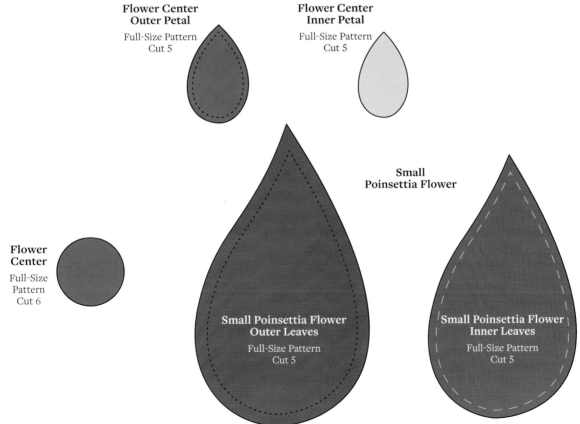

**Flower Center
Outer Petal**

Full-Size Pattern
Cut 5

**Flower Center
Inner Petal**

Full-Size Pattern
Cut 5

Small
Poinsettia Flower

**Flower
Center**

Full-Size
Pattern
Cut 6

**Small Poinsettia Flower
Outer Leaves**

Full-Size Pattern
Cut 5

**Small Poinsettia Flower
Inner Leaves**

Full-Size Pattern
Cut 5

Felt Cone Trees

These tabletop felt trees radiate homespun warmth and elegance. They're deceivingly easy to create. Strips of felt are folded, stitched, and then cut into loops. The cut strips are simply wrapped and glued around a foam cone base.

Dimensions

Small tree is 8¾ inches high×4½ inches diameter at the base
Big tree is 11¾ inches high×5¾ inches diameter at the base

WHAT YOU NEED

Plastic foam cones such as Styrofoam • 1 yard of beige/natural 100% wool felt such as National Nonwovens • ½- to ¾-inch felt beads • Off-white thread • Floral glue such as Floracraft glue • Straight pins • Hot-glue gun and glue sticks • Rotary cutter • Straight edge and cutting mat • Sewing machine • Purchased felt beads in desired colors • Purchased felt star for topper

WHAT YOU DO

1. Use a rotary cutter and straight edge to cut the felt into 5-inch-wide strips of felt. Utilize the full length of the felt; you'll cut the strip apart when you wrap it around the cone in Step 4.

2. Fold the top 1½ inches down to the center of the strip, then pin the folded portion in place. Fold the bottom 1½ inches up to the center of the strip and pin it in place. Your flat strip should be transformed into two folded portions with a center channel where the edges meet. Make two seams in this center channel, one to hold the top edge in place and the other to hold the bottom edge.

3. Separate the folded sections into loops with sharp scissors. Cut straight slits that are ⅓ to ½ inch apart. Be careful not to cut into the seams.

4. Starting at the base of the cone, wrap the end loopy strip around the foam cone. Where the strip overlaps the beginning, cut the measured length off the strip. Set this first piece aside and then repeat the process to measure and cut strips to wrap up the rest of the tree. **Note:** The closer you position the loop strips around the tree, the fuller it will be.

5. Once you've cut all the strips, apply foam glue to the center channel at the back of the first (bottom) strip. Wrap the strip around the plastic foam and then use straight pins to hold it in place, one at the beginning and end of the strip and the other in the center. Repeat the process to glue and pin the remaining strips in place. Push the top loops down and out of the way before gluing and wrapping each new strip.

6. Use a 3-inch section of the loop strip for the tree top. Roll up one end of the strip, then use a little hot glue to hold the center of the rolled up portion together. Position the rolled-up portion over the cone top. Use foam glue to attach the base to the top of the cone. Use a few pins to hold the top in place.

7. Glue a felt star to the top of the tree. Tuck small and large felt beads between the loops all around the tree. Once you're pleased with the arrangement, hot-glue the felt beads in place.

Loops of felt are tucked together to form the softest of Christmas trees. Make a couple trees or an entire forest of these sweet little trees to add homespun charm to any table or mantel.

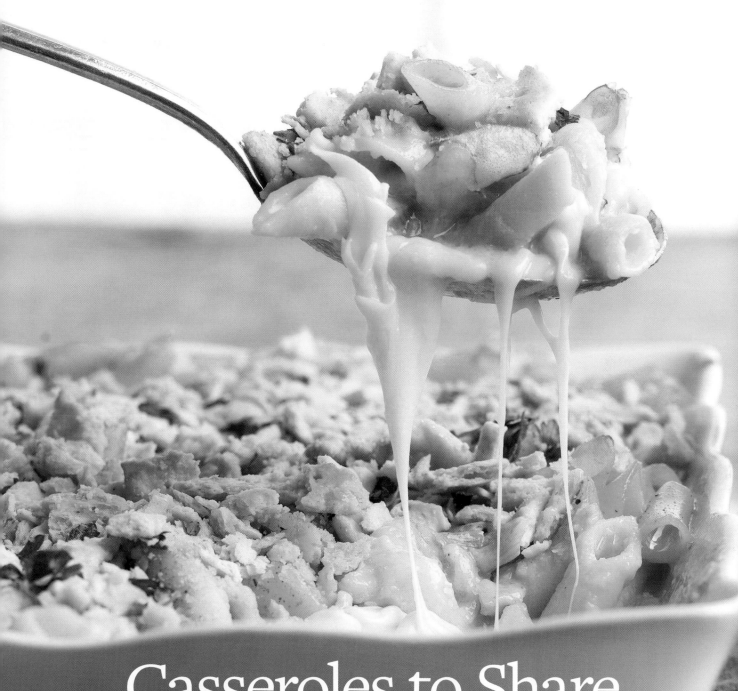

Casseroles to Share

A hot and bubbly meal baked in one dish is something everyone craves at holiday gatherings. These deliciously intriguing recipes are companyworthy in both flavor and appearance.

Savory Beef and Sweet Potato Pies

For a lighter version of these savory pies, use ground turkey or chicken in place of the beef.

WHAT YOU NEED
3 pounds sweet potatoes (4 to 5 medium), peeled and cut into 1-inch pieces
2 tablespoons finely snipped fresh rosemary
¼ cup butter, cut up
¾ teaspoon salt
½ cup mascarpone cheese
1½ pounds lean ground beef
2 cups finely chopped carrots (4 medium)
½ cup chopped onion (1 medium)
½ cup dry red wine or beef broth
¼ cup all-purpose flour
1 14.5-ounce can beef broth
2 cups frozen peas, thawed
1 tablespoon soy sauce
¼ teaspoon ground nutmeg
   Nonstick cooking spray

WHAT YOU DO
1. Preheat oven to 400°F. In a Dutch oven cook sweet potatoes and rosemary, covered, in enough boiling lightly salted water to cover for 15 to 20 minutes or until sweet potatoes are tender; drain. Return mixture to Dutch oven. Mash with a potato masher or an electric mixer on low until smooth. Add butter and ½ teaspoon of the salt; gradually beat in mascarpone cheese until light and fluffy. Set aside.
2. In an extra-large skillet cook ground beef, carrots, and onion over medium-high heat until meat is browned and carrots are crisp-tender. Drain off fat.
3. Stir wine into meat mixture. Cook and stir about 2 minutes or until liquid is evaporated. Sprinkle with flour; cook and stir for 2 minutes more. Add broth. Cook and stir until mixture is slightly thickened and bubbly. Stir in peas, soy sauce, nutmeg, and remaining ¼ teaspoon salt.
4. Lightly coat eight 10- to 12-ounce ramekins or a 3-quart rectangular baking dish with cooking spray. Divide meat mixture evenly among ramekins or transfer to baking dish. Top with mashed sweet potatoes. If using ramekins, place them in a shallow baking pan or roasting pan.
5. Bake 15 to 20 minutes for ramekins or about 20 minutes for 3-quart dish or until heated through and starting to brown. Makes 8 servings.

Turkey Meatballs in Pesto Pasta Pie

You probably already have nearly all of the ingredients for this tasty spaghetti casserole in your pantry and fridge.

WHAT YOU NEED
5 ounces dried spaghetti, preferably whole grain spaghetti
6 tablespoons purchased basil pesto
1 egg, lightly beaten

   Nonstick cooking spray
1 cup ricotta cheese
1 16-ounce package frozen turkey meatballs
1 cup tomato-base pasta sauce with mushrooms
½ cup sliced pitted Kalamata olives
2 tablespoons water
½ cup shredded pizza cheese (2 ounces)
   Snipped fresh basil (optional)

WHAT YOU DO
1. Cook spaghetti according to package directions; drain. Stir in 4 tablespoons of the pesto and the egg; set aside.
2. Coat a 9-inch pie plate with cooking spray. Press spaghetti mixture onto bottom and up sides of prepared pie plate, forming a crust. In a small bowl combine ricotta and the remaining 2 tablespoons pesto; spread over the top and up the sides of the pasta crust.
3. Preheat oven to 350°F. In a medium saucepan stir together frozen turkey meatballs, pasta sauce, olives, and the water. Bring to boiling, stirring occasionally; reduce heat. Simmer, covered, about 5 minutes or just until meatballs are heated through, stirring twice. Spoon meatball mixture into pasta crust. Cover pie loosely with foil.
4. Bake for 25 minutes. Sprinkle with pizza cheese. Bake, uncovered, about 5 minutes more or until heated through. If desired, sprinkle with snipped fresh basil. Makes 6 servings.

Short Rib Ragoût with Polenta Croutons

This dish gets even better as it chills in the fridge because the flavors of the ragoût have time to meld.

WHAT YOU NEED

3   pounds boneless beef short ribs
    Salt
    Ground black pepper
2   to 3 tablespoons olive oil
2   medium onions, thinly sliced
6   cloves garlic, minced
3   medium carrots, halved lengthwise and sliced
    (1½ cups)
1   cup coarsely chopped celery (2 stalks)
1   14.5-ounce can reduced-sodium beef broth
1½ cups dry red wine, such as Merlot or Cabernet
    Sauvignon
1   6-ounce can tomato paste
4   sprigs fresh thyme
1   8-ounce package cremini mushrooms, quartered
    (thickly slice larger caps)
1   recipe Firm Polenta
1   tablespoon snipped fresh Italian parsley
    or basil (optional)

WHAT YOU DO

1. Preheat oven to 325°F. Sprinkle ribs with salt and pepper. In a 6- to 8-quart oven-going Dutch oven heat 1 tablespoon of the olive oil over medium heat. Brown ribs, half at a time if necessary, in the hot oil, turning to brown all sides; remove ribs and set aside. In the same Dutch oven cook onions and garlic for 2 minutes, adding another 1 tablespoon of the oil if needed. Add carrots and celery; cook about 5 minutes more or until vegetables are tender.
2. Return ribs to Dutch oven with the vegetables. Stir in broth, wine, tomato paste, and thyme sprigs. Bring to boiling. Cover; bake for 1½ hours. Stir in mushrooms. Bake, uncovered, for 45 to 60 minutes more or until ribs are tender and sauce is slightly thickened. Cool for 30 minutes. Discard thyme sprigs. Season to taste with additional salt and pepper.
3. Transfer rib mixture to a large airtight container. Cover and chill for at least 8 hours or up to 3 days.
4. Preheat oven to 375°F. Lightly grease a 3-quart rectangular baking dish; set aside. Using a spoon, remove any fat from surface of the sauce. Spoon ribs and sauce into prepared baking dish. If desired, cut short ribs into smaller portions. Run a thin metal spatula around the edges of the Firm Polenta in the loaf pan. Remove polenta loaf from pan and cut into 1-inch cubes. Arrange cubes evenly over the ribs and sauce in the baking dish. Brush the cubes with the remaining 1 tablespoon olive oil. Bake, uncovered, about 1 hour or until ribs and sauce are heated through and polenta is lightly browned. If desired, sprinkle with parsley. Makes 8 servings.
Firm Polenta: In a medium saucepan bring 2½ cups water to boiling. In a medium bowl stir together 1 cup coarse-ground cornmeal, 1 cup cold water, and 1 teaspoon salt. Slowly add cornmeal mixture to the boiling water, stirring constantly. Cook and stir until mixture returns to boiling. Reduce heat to medium-low. Cook for 25 to 30 minutes or until mixture is thick, stirring frequently and adjusting heat as needed to maintain a slow boil. Pour into an ungreased 8×4×2-inch loaf pan. Cover and chill for at least 8 hours or up to 3 days.

For safe toting, tightly cover a piping hot casserole with foil. Then wrap the dish in layers of newspaper and kitchen towels and transport in an insulated container.

Black Bean and Root Vegetable Enchiladas

This pleasantly spicy meatless dish will bring the heat on a cold winter night. Double the recipe if you're planning to serve a large group.

WHAT YOU NEED

2   14.5-ounce cans fire-roasted diced tomatoes with garlic, undrained
1   cup bottled salsa
1   tablespoon ground ancho chile pepper or regular chili powder
1   to 2 teaspoons unsweetened cocoa powder
    Salt
    Ground black pepper
    Nonstick cooking spray
8   7- to 8-inch flour tortillas
2   teaspoons olive oil or vegetable oil
⅓   cup chopped onion (1 small)
1½ cups peeled and chopped assorted root vegetables, such as parsnip, turnip, rutabaga, sweet potato, and/or carrot
1   teaspoon ground cumin
1   15-ounce can black beans, rinsed and drained
1¼ cups shredded Mexican cheese blend or Monterey Jack cheese (5 ounces)
¼   cup snipped fresh cilantro
¼   cup Mexican crema or ¼ cup sour cream mixed with 1 tablespoon water
    Bottled salsa, Mexican crema, and/or shredded Mexican-style four-cheese blend or Monterey Jack cheese (optional)

WHAT YOU DO

1. In a medium saucepan combine tomatoes, 1 cup salsa, ground ancho pepper, and cocoa powder. Bring to boiling; reduce heat. Simmer, uncovered, about 10 minutes or until slightly thickened, stirring occasionally and mashing with the back of a spoon. Season to taste with salt and black pepper; set aside.

2. Meanwhile, preheat oven to 350°F. Coat a 2-quart rectangular baking dish with cooking spray; set aside. Stack tortillas; wrap tightly in foil. Bake about 10 minutes or until warm.

3. In a large skillet heat oil over medium heat. Add onion; cook for 2 minutes. Add root vegetables and cumin; cook and stir for 3 to 4 minutes or until vegetables are crisp-tender. Remove from heat. Stir in half of the tomato mixture, the beans, ¾ cup of the cheese, and 2 tablespoons of the cilantro.

4. Divide bean mixture among warm tortillas; roll up tortillas. Arrange rolled tortillas, seam sides down, in the prepared baking dish.

5. Spoon the remaining tomato mixture over enchiladas. Sprinkle with the remaining ½ cup cheese. Bake, uncovered, for 15 to 20 minutes or until heated through.

6. Drizzle with ¼ cup crema. Bake, uncovered, for 5 minutes more. Sprinkle with remaining 2 tablespoons cilantro. If desired, serve with additional salsa, Mexican crema, and/or cheese. Makes 4 to 6 servings.

To Make Ahead: Prepare as directed through Step 4. Cover baking dish with foil. Transfer the remaining tomato mixture to an airtight container; cover. Place the remaining ½ cup cheese and the remaining 2 tablespoons cilantro in separate plastic bags; seal bags. Chill enchiladas, tomato mixture, cheese, and cilantro for 2 to 24 hours. To serve, preheat oven to 350°F. Spoon the remaining tomato mixture over enchiladas. Bake, covered, for 20 minutes. Sprinkle with the remaining ½ cup cheese. Bake, uncovered, about 20 minutes more or until heated through. Continue as directed in Step 6.

For best flavor and food safety, casseroles should be heated to 160°F. Test doneness by inserting an instant-read thermometer at an angle into the center of the dish.

Sausage Pizza Slab Pie

Play with the top layer of dough for an easy lattice crust or cut out holiday shapes to cover the top.

WHAT YOU NEED
3   13.8-ounce packages refrigerated pizza dough
8   ounces bulk hot or sweet Italian sausage, cooked and drained
2   cups shredded fresh spinach leaves
1   cup canned pizza sauce or bottled pasta sauce
1   cup quartered thawed frozen artichoke hearts
½   cup sliced pitted ripe olives or Kalamata olives
⅓   cup slivered red onion
2   cups shredded Italian-blend cheese (8 ounces)
1   cup shredded Parmesan cheese (4 ounces)

WHAT YOU DO
1. Preheat oven to 375°F. Lightly grease a 15×10×1-inch baking pan. Unroll 2 packages of the pizza dough and place in the prepared baking pan, overlapping long ends slightly and pressing them together to make one sheet of dough. Using your hands, press dough to cover bottom and sides of pan. Set aside.
2. In a medium bowl stir together sausage, spinach, sauce, artichoke hearts, olives, and onion. Spread evenly over dough in pan. Sprinkle with Italian-blend cheese.
3. Unroll the remaining package of pizza dough on a lightly floured surface. Roll out dough into a 15-inch-long rectangle; cut lengthwise into 10 strips. Place 5 of the strips lengthwise on top of filling. Give pan a quarter turn; arrange the remaining 5 strips perpendicular to the first

strips on filling, trimming to fit as necessary. Sprinkle dough strips with Parmesan cheese.
4. Bake for 35 to 40 minutes or until crust is golden. If necessary to prevent overbrowning, cover crust edges loosely with foil for the last 10 minutes of baking. Makes 15 servings.

Ravioli Lasagna with Chianti Sauce

Chianti is a dry, boldly flavored red wine named for the Chianti region of Tuscany, Italy. Its robust character adds richness and depth to the highly seasoned sauce in this dish.

WHAT YOU NEED
¼   cup olive oil
½   cup chopped onion (1 medium)
3   cloves garlic, minced
1   28-ounce can crushed tomatoes, undrained
1   cup Chianti or other full-bodied dry red wine
1   tablespoon dried oregano, crushed
1   teaspoon salt
¼   to ½ teaspoon crushed red pepper
1   12-ounce package cooked Italian-style poultry sausages, halved lengthwise and cut into ½-inch pieces
12 ounces fresh cremini mushrooms or button mushrooms, sliced
1   7-ounce jar roasted red sweet peppers, drained and coarsely chopped
½   cup snipped fresh basil
2   9-ounce packages refrigerated cheese ravioli
1   8-ounce package shredded mozzarella cheese (2 cups)

WHAT YOU DO
1. For Chianti tomato sauce, in a large saucepan heat 1 teaspoon of the olive oil over medium heat. Add onion and garlic; cook about 3 minutes or until onion is tender. Add tomatoes, Chianti, oregano, salt, and crushed red pepper. Bring to boiling; reduce heat. Simmer, uncovered, about 10 minutes or until slightly reduced.
2. Meanwhile, in a very large skillet heat 1 tablespoon of the olive oil over medium heat. Add sausage pieces and mushrooms; cook until mushrooms are tender. Stir in roasted red peppers and basil; set aside.
3. Spoon one-fourth of the Chianti tomato sauce into a 3-quart rectangular baking dish. Arrange 1 package of the ravioli on top. Spoon half of the sausage-mushroom mixture over. Spoon another one-fourth of the sauce over sausage-mushroom mixture in baking dish. Top with half of the mozzarella cheese. Spoon another one-fourth of the sauce over cheese. Repeat layers with the remaining ravioli, sausage-mushroom mixture, sauce, and cheese.
4. Preheat oven to 375°F. Bake, covered, for 35 minutes. Uncover. Bake about 5 minutes more or until cheese is bubbly and lasagna is heated through. Let stand for 10 minutes before serving. Makes 8 servings.

Shrimp Fondue Casserole

You'll get the best melting results by shredding the Swiss and Gruyère cheeses just before they're ready to go into the sauce.

WHAT YOU NEED

12 ounces fresh or frozen peeled, deveined uncooked small shrimp, halved lengthwise
    Nonstick cooking spray
12 ounces dried mostaccioli pasta or elbow macaroni
3   cups shredded Swiss cheese (12 ounces)
2½ cups shredded Gruyère cheese (10 ounces)
⅓   cup all-purpose flour
3   cloves garlic, minced
1   14.5-ounce can chicken broth
1   cup dry white wine
1½ teaspoons seafood seasoning
8   ounces Swiss cheese, cubed
½   cup sliced green onions (4)
1¾ cups crushed saltine crackers (36)
1   tablespoon snipped fresh parsley
3   tablespoons butter, cut up

WHAT YOU DO

1. Thaw shrimp, if frozen. Preheat oven to 350°F. Coat a 3-quart rectangular baking dish with cooking spray; set aside. Cook pasta according to package directions; drain. Return pasta to pan; set aside.

2. Meanwhile, in a large bowl combine the shredded Swiss cheese, Gruyère cheese, flour, and garlic. Toss to combine. In a large saucepan heat broth and wine over medium heat just until bubbles form around edge of pan. Add cheese mixture, 1 cup at a time, whisking constantly after each addition until cheese melts. (Mixture may not be completely smooth at this point.) Do not boil. Remove from heat. Stir in seafood seasoning.

3. Pour cheese mixture over pasta; stir gently to combine. Fold in the cubed Swiss cheese, shrimp, and green onions. Spoon pasta mixture into prepared dish.

4. In a small bowl combine crushed crackers and parsley. Sprinkle mixture evenly over top of pasta; dot with butter. Bake for 35 to 40 minutes or until bubbly and topping is golden. Makes 8 servings.

To Make Ahead: Prepare as directed, except stir ½ cup milk into cheese mixture at the end of Step 2. Cool cheese mixture and pasta slightly before combining. Continue with Step 3. Do not prepare or top with cracker mixture. Cover casserole; chill for up to 24 hours. To serve, preheat oven to 350°F. If necessary, stir up to ½ cup additional milk into casserole to moisten. (If necessary, turn mixture into a larger bowl to combine.) Prepare cracker mixture; sprinkle on top of cheese mixture. Dot with butter. Bake for 1 hour or until bubbly and topping is golden.

When cooking dry pasta for use in a casserole, check the cooking time range on the package and cook for the shorter time. Pasta will continue to soften as the casserole bakes.

Let It Snow

Every winter, nature blankets the land in layers of icy beauty.
You can add the season's shimmer and cool palette to your
own displays with trims of glitter and frosty paints and papers.

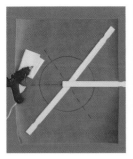

Wooden Snowflake Decor

Cast a magical spell over a door with a supersize snowflake made from painted crafts sticks and other wooden shapes. Tuck a few fresh evergreen branches behind the snowflake and secure with florist's wire to introduce the sweet scent of pine. Then scatter these wooden snowflakes behind a bed or on a stair railing to add winter beauty all through the house.

WHAT YOU NEED

Dinner plate • Marker • Kraft paper or newspaper • 6 large paint stirrers • Small, medium, and large wooden crafts sticks • Bags of wooden crafts shapes in squares, triangles, and circles, such as Woodsies • Wood coffee stirrers • Hot-glue gun and glue sticks • Adhesive or tacky glue • Scissors • White spray paint • Textured paint such as Krylon Make It Stone White Onyx • Ribbon

WHAT YOU DO

1. Spread out materials on a large, flat work surface. Work in assembly-line fashion, completing the same step on each snowflake before moving to the next step. This simplifies the process and gives the glue time to dry between steps. Use a dinner plate and a marker to trace a circle onto a piece of kraft paper. Divide the circle evenly into sixths. Use this template as a guide for centering each snowflake.
2. Each snowflake base is made from a minimum of three long sticks, which are created by gluing together either two paint stirrers or two large wood crafts sticks for smaller Stick Snowflakes. Overlap stirrers or sticks by ½ inch in the middle for support, ensuring the stirrers or sticks are straight. Lay the long stirrers or sticks over the lines of the kraft paper template, gluing at the center; let dry.
3. Add wooden shapes, cutting to fit with scissors if needed, to create snowflake patterns you like. If angling two crafts sticks to create a fan shape, cut the ends at a 45-degree angle so they both fit neatly on top of the long stick and under a shape.
4. When designs are completed and glued together, let dry. Then spray-paint the snowflakes white. For a textured finish, apply textured paint and then top with white spray paint. Let dry. To hang, attach ribbon to the back of the finished snowflake.

Like real snowflakes, the patterns are endless! Show off your best snowflake-making skills by hanging these beauties on a door, behind a bed, or dangling from a stair railing.

Drifts of Snow Stockings

Gently scalloped cuffs made of white fabric create winter landscapes on this collection of wintery stockings.

Note: Stockings can be made from pattern provided or cuffs added to purchased stockings. Choose a cuff from the patterns, refer to photo, or design your own cuff pattern.

WHAT YOU NEED

Tracing paper • Pencil • Scissors • ½ yard of blue or white fabric such as velveteen for stocking body • ¼ yard white fabric such as satin or polished cotton for cuff • 10-inch piece of silver ribbon for loop • Matching sewing thread

WHAT YOU DO

1. Enlarge stocking and desired cuff patterns, below, onto tracing paper and cut out. Cut patterns from appropriate fabrics.
2. Sew stocking body pieces with right sides together, using a ¼-inch seam, leaving top straight edge open. Clip curves.
3. Stitch short ends of cuff, right sides together. Pin right side of cuff to wrong side of stocking. Stitch with ¼-inch seam. Turn cuff to outside, turning stocking right side out. Press lightly.
4. Stitch short ends of cuff lining, right sides together. With right sides together, pin cuff lining over cuff front. Stitch around cuff scallops. Turn and press.
5. Tack ribbon to cuff for hanging.

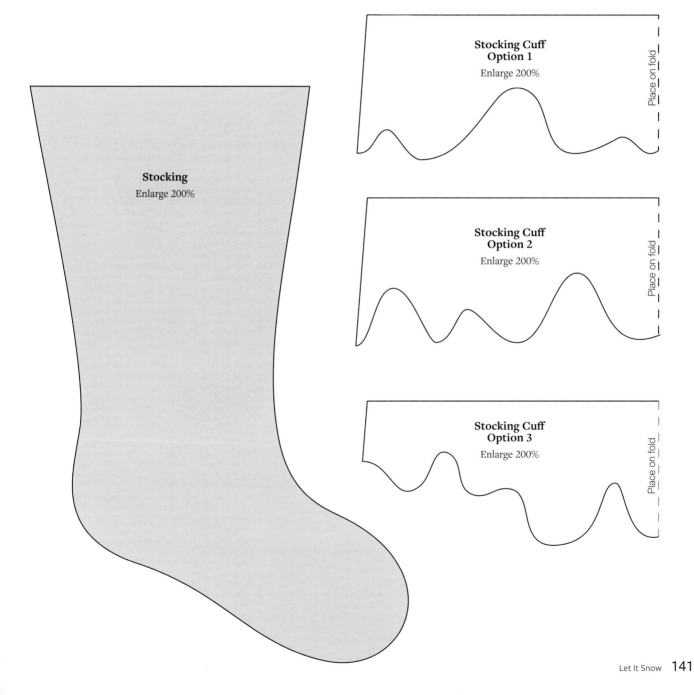

Stocking
Enlarge 200%

Stocking Cuff Option 1
Enlarge 200%
Place on fold

Stocking Cuff Option 2
Enlarge 200%
Place on fold

Stocking Cuff Option 3
Enlarge 200%
Place on fold

Embroidered Snowflake Pillow

Every snowflake is a work of art and a thing of beauty—ideal inspiration for winter crafting. This simple snowflake embroiders quickly with yarn and a chunky chain stitch. Punctuate the design with your collection of vintage buttons. The warm felt background and chenille backing are soft to the touch, creating an accent pillow that can be enjoyed all winter long.

WHAT YOU NEED

16-inch square of blue wool felt • Chenille fabric • 14-inch pillow form • ¾-inch button • ½-inch button • Organic yarn • Off-white thread • Embroidery needle • Rotary cutter • Mat and straight edge • Sewing machine • Straight pins

WHAT YOU DO

1. Referring to the illustrated stitch diagram, below left, start embroidering the snowflake and sewing buttons onto the blue wool felt square. Use a length of yarn and a darning needle to stitch the large button to the center of the felt square. The snowflake has four long arms and four shorter arms; each grouping creates a large X that intersects the center button.

2. For the large arm, starting beside the large button make three connected ½-inch-long chain stitches. Cap the end of the last stitch with two ½-inch-long diagonal stitches. Sew a ½-inch button in the center of the diagonal stitches. Make a single stitch just above the button; cap this stitch with two more ¾-inch diagonal stitches. Sew a second ½-inch button in the center of the diagonal stitches. End this arm with a single ¼-inch straight stitch above the button. Repeat this sequence three more times, making right angles out from the center button.

3. For the smaller arm, starting beside the large button make a single ½-inch chain stitch and cap it with two ¾-inch diagonal stitches. Sew a ½-inch button between the diagonal stitches. Make two connected chain stitches above the button. Make two ¾-inch diagonal stitches at the beginning and end of the chain. Sew a ½-inch button above the diagonal stitches, then end this arm with a single ¼-inch straight stitch. Repeat the sequence three more times, making diagonal angles out from the center button.

4. Trim the finished felt square and prepare the chenille backing. Using the mat, straight edge, and rotary cutter, trim the embroidered felt to a 14½-inch square. This the perfect time to straighten up the snowflake if it unintentionally migrated to one side of the square. Next cut two chenille rectangles, one 9×14½ inches and another 10×14½ inches. These pieces will overlap to cover the back of the pillow. Turn under ¼ inch of the 14½-inch edge of each piece, pin, and then machine stitch. This will prevent the open ends from fraying when you insert and remove the pillow.

5. Pin the back pieces over the square and machine stitch around the outside edge

6. Placing right sides together, place the chenille pieces over the pillow front. Position the finished edges toward the center of the pillow. The chenille pieces will overlap by approximately 3½ inches. Pin the outside edges together and then machine stitch around the outside edge. Trim away excess fabric and turn the pillow right side out. Insert pillow form.

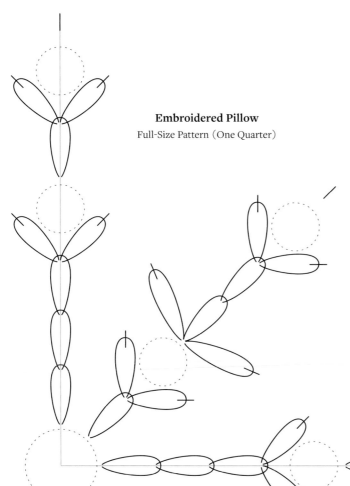

Embroidered Pillow
Full-Size Pattern (One Quarter)

A Midwinter's Dream

Invite winter's beauty inside—but leave behind the chill—with this delicate feather tree. Light and lacy, its branches bear the shimmering elegance of the season. Fanciful birds, icicles, crystalline snowflakes, and Santa boots will have you humming "White Christmas" whenever you pass by.

Beaded Icicle Jewel

WHAT YOU NEED

Terry cloth hand towel • Steel bench block • 18-gauge 6-inch silver-plated stickpin • Plastic-head mallet • Two 6-mm Czech fire-polished round beads • Two 8-mm Czech fire-polished round or rondel beads • 3 blown-glass beads (1 large and 2 small, or 2 large and 1 small) • Three 8×10 mm faceted-glass bicone beads • Silver-plated bead caps, 6-mm, or 8-mm (depending on the size of the bead) • Pliers (chain-nose, round-nose, and flat-nose) • Flush-cut wire cutters • 16-gauge sterling-silver dead-soft wire • ¾-inch-diameter wooden dowel • *For product information, see page 160.*

WHAT YOU DO

1. Fold the hand towel in quarters and set the bench block on the towel. Place the silver-plated stickpin on the bench block and pound it with the mallet until it will not easily bend.
2. Thread the following beads onto the stickpin, adding bead caps on each side of the large blown-glass beads: 6-mm round, 8-mm round (or rondel), 6-mm round, blown-glass bead, bicone, 8-mm round (or rondel), bicone, blown-glass bead, bicone, blown-glass bead.
3. Use chain-nose pliers to bend the wire at the top of the icicle at a 45-degree angle. Cut wire ⅜ inch from the bend. Use round-nose pliers to create a loop.
4. To attach the hook, use the wire cutters to cut a 3¾-inch piece of sterling-silver wire and shape ornament hook.
5. With the chain-nose pliers in one hand and the flat-nose pliers in the other, open the bottom loop of the finished hook. Thread the open loop onto the loop of the beaded icicle; close the loop.

Snowflake Charm

WHAT YOU NEED

6-inch-wide snowflake form • 6 seed beads (Size 11) • 6 seed beads (Size 6 or 8) • 6-mm or 8-mm Czech fire-polished round beads (12 each of two colors) • 6 blown-glass oval beads • Pliers (chain-nose, round-nose, and flat-nose) • Flush-cut wire cutters • 16-gauge sterling-silver dead-soft wire • *For product information, see page 160.*

WHAT YOU DO

1. Thread one wire of the snowflake form with beads as follows: Size 11 seed bead, Size 6 (or Size 8) seed bead, round bead (color 1), round bead (color 2), blown-glass bead, round bead (color 2), round bead (color 1). Using the chain-nose pliers, bend the wire just above the last bead toward you at a 45-degree angle.
2. Using the wire cutters, trim the wire ⅜ inch from the bend. Use the round-nose pliers to bend exposed ⅜-inch length of wire into a loop. Close the loop tight using the flat-nose or chain-nose pliers. Repeat for the remaining snowflake wire.
3. Using the wire cutters, cut a 3¾-inch piece of sterling-silver wire. With the chain-nose pliers in one hand and the flat-nose pliers in the other, open the bottom loop. Thread the open loop onto the loop of the beaded snowflake; close the loop.

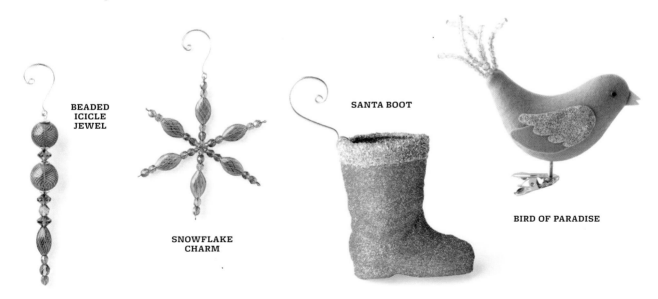

BEADED ICICLE JEWEL

SNOWFLAKE CHARM

SANTA BOOT

BIRD OF PARADISE

Bird of Paradise

WHAT YOU NEED

9×14-inch piece of aqua (or avocado) wool felt • Clear-drying fabrics glue • Plastic putty knife • Ultrafine glitter in color to match the felt • Tracing paper • Fusible knit interfacing • Water-soluble marking pen • Paper-backed fusible web such as Heat-n-Bond Lite • Scrap of gray wool felt • 24-gauge silver crafts wire • Wire cutters • Pliers (round-nose and chain-nose) • Darning needle • 45 4-mm round beads in two colors for tail • 2 beads for eyes • Crafts glue • Polyester fiberfill • Silver bird-leg clip

WHAT YOU DO

1. To make the glittered felt for the top wings, cut a 3-inch square of aqua (or avocado) felt. Apply fabrics glue to one side of the felt using the putty knife.

2. Place the felt square, glue side up, on a sheet of paper and sprinkle with glitter in color that matches the felt. Shake the excess glitter onto the paper. Set the felt aside; let the glue dry. Use the paper to funnel excess glitter back into the container.

3. Enlarge and trace the pattern, below, onto tracing paper and cut out. Fuse a 5×8-inch piece of fusible knit interfacing to a slightly larger piece of felt. Cut out two body pieces from the interfaced felt, reversing the pattern for one. Mark eye placement and all dots using the water-soluble pen.

4. From felt, cut two bottom wings, reversing the pattern for one.

5. Fuse a 1-inch square of paper-backed fusible web to the gray felt. Trace the beak pattern onto the paper side of the webbing and cut out. Remove paper backing and fuse back to a second piece of gray felt. Cut out beak.

6. Cut two top wings from glittered felt, reversing one.

7. Cut five 14-inch lengths of wire. Make a tight coil in the end, bending each coil at a 90-degree angle. Thread eight to 12 beads on the wire. Set aside.

8. Using ¼-inch seams, stay-stitch along the bottom edge of the each body piece between two small dots. With right sides together, baste the beak to one body piece. Sew body pieces with right sides together, leaving the area between the small dots and across tail unstitched. Trim seams. Match the top and bottom seam lines at the tail; sew across the tail ⅜ inch from the end. Turn body right side out.

9. Using the darning needle, make three holes at the end of the tail. Insert the straight end of the beaded wire into each hole, exiting the wires at the opening in the bird. Turn the tail wrong side out and twist the tail wires together on the inside. Turn the tail right side out.

10. Stuff the head and tail with fiberfill. Insert the leg clip. Pin opening closed. Glue eyes to sides of bird head.

11. Fuse the fusible-web wing pieces to the bottom felt wings. Remove paper backing. Place the top wings over the bottom wings. With the glittered sides down, fuse together the wing pieces. Blind-stitch the wings to the bird.

Santa Boot

WHAT YOU NEED

Brown paper bag • Strong crafts glue • Papier-mâché Santa boots (available at crafts stores or see Sources page 160) • Acrylic paints in metallic silver, green or aqua blue • Paintbrush • Silver and green or blue crafts glitter • Darning needle • Flush-cut wire cutters • 16-gauge sterling-silver wire • Pliers (round-nose, chain-nose, and flat-nose)

WHAT YOU DO

1. To paint the boots, tear a 1-inch square from the brown paper bag and glue it to the inside of the boot at the upper back edge (for ornament hook reinforcement). Paint the outside of the boot with green or blue. Paint the boot trim and interior with silver paint.

2. To add the glitter, using a paintbrush, apply glue to the outside of the boot, excluding the trim. Hold the boot over a sheet of paper and, while the glue is wet, sprinkle the boot with glitter that matches the paint color. Shake the excess glitter onto the paper. Use the paper to funnel the excess glitter back into the container. Let the boot dry.

3. In the same way, apply glue to the boot trim and interior; sprinkle with silver glitter. Let dry. Reapply glue to the trim and sprinkle with the glitter. Let dry.

4. Push the darning needle through the center back of the boot trim to create a hole for the hanging hook.

5. Using the wire cutters, cut a 4½-inch piece of the sterling-silver wire. With the chain-nose pliers in one hand and the flat-nose pliers in the other, open the bottom loop of the finished hook. Thread the open loop through the hole in the boot trim; close the loop.

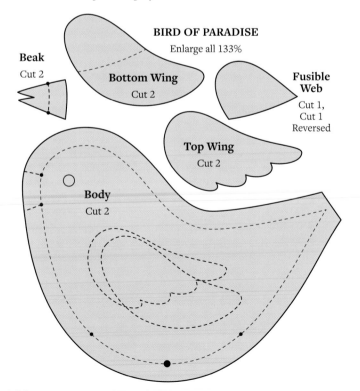

BIRD OF PARADISE

Enlarge all 133%

Beak
Cut 2

Bottom Wing
Cut 2

Fusible Web
Cut 1,
Cut 1
Reversed

Top Wing
Cut 2

Body
Cut 2

Paper snowflakes in cool winter hues are die-cut and layered to create a lovely wreath. Groups of jewels are added to the snowflakes for added sparkle.

Shimmering Snowflake Wreath

Snowflakes cut from winter-white and shiny teal cardstock are layered and jeweled to create a stunning winter wreath.

WHAT YOU NEED

12-inch flat foam wreath such as Styrofoam • Shimmer-style cardstock in shades of white and teal • Variety of large snowflake dies and punches • Circle punches • Wide ribbon • Trimmer • Scissors • Adhesive, including strong double-sided tape and foam dots • Adhesive jewels

WHAT YOU DO

1. Trace the wreath form onto cardstock and cut a circle to cover the front of the wreath; adhere with double-sided tape adhesive. Wrap wide ribbon around the wreath form and knot at top.

2. Die-cut and punch a variety of snowflakes from cardstock. If snowflakes have cutout areas, punch circles from contrasting cardstock and adhere to back side. Punch small circles to adhere to the fronts of some snowflakes.

3. Arrange snowflakes around the wreath, balancing styles and colors. Adhere the snowflakes to the wreath form using foam dots under some of the snowflakes for dimension. Add layers, extending over the edges of the wreath form. Adhere jewels to some of the snowflakes for sparkle.

Sweet Settings

Deck your table in style this holiday season with table settings
that are sure to bring smiles. From elegant to homespun—your
table will add seasonal sparkle to your holiday celebration.

Holly Leaf Table Setting

Let a simple holly leaf be the inspiration for an elegant Christmas Eve dinner. Choose colors in traditional red and green to set a table that says "Merry Christmas!"

WHAT YOU DO

Choose a cream or white table cloth and white dishes trimmed in red or green. Place the soup bowl on top of the dinner plate. Fold the napkin into quarters and then tuck the sides back. Trace the patterns, right and below, onto green print cardstock and cut out. Starting at the back of the napkin, wrap a piece of red satin ribbon around the napkin, crisscrossing at the front. Use double-sided tape to secure. Adhere the leaf stem and leaves to the front of the ribbon using double-sided tape. Add three red jewels in the center of the holly leaves. Place on top of soup bowl.

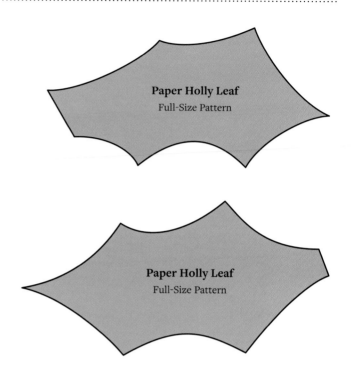

Paper Holly Leaf
Full-Size Pattern

Paper Holly Leaf
Full-Size Pattern

Paper Holly Leaf
Full-Size Pattern

Ring the Bells Tablescape

Gather your most elegant dishes and flatware and make them sing by adding a single metallic jingle bell.

WHAT YOU DO

Choose a white tablecloth and monochromatic dishes. Stack the salad plate on the dinner plate. Thread a narrow white satin ribbon through the top of a large silver jingle bell. Fold the napkin in quarters and then into eighths. Tie the ribbon and the jingle bell around the napkin. Lay the napkin on the plate. Decorate the table with clear glass ornaments cascading down the tablecloth.

Pretty Paper Place Setting

You can create almost anything from the wonderful array of scrapbook papers available to crafters today. Try your hand at making paper place mats with matching napkin rings, place cards, and even a bright and sparkling centerpiece.

WHAT YOU NEED

Patterned paper in a variety of coordinated colors/designs • Matching cardstock •Decorative-edge paper or border punch • Ribbon • Twine or cording • Circle dies and/or punches in concentric sizes (large circles in our setting measure 2½ inches and 2⅛ inches) • Holiday dies and/or punches • Glass vase and small votive containers • Small candles • Beads or mini ornaments to fill large vase • Scissors • Scoring tool • Printer or stamps to create names for place cards • Adhesive, including strong double-sided tape and foam dots

WHAT YOU DO

For place mats

1. Create place mat by using purchased decorative-edged paper or create your own by punching cardstock with a specialty border punch. Place contrasting cardstock behind any openings in the place mat and add punched circles to the front side.
2. Adhere the round place mat to a full sheet of patterned paper if desired.

For place cards

1. Cut cardstock to 4×4½ inches and score at 2¼ inches. Fold in half to create place card "tent." Cut a smaller piece of patterned paper to fit the front of the place card.
2. Print or stamp guest's name on a strip of cardstock a bit wider than the place card. Notch one end with scissors to create a banner, then adhere the strip to the place card. Cut circles from matching cardstock and adhere to front of place card with foam dots. Adhere a holiday die cut or punched piece to the circles. Embellish with ribbon or twine.

For napkin rings

1. Cut and layer strips of patterned paper to fit around your napkins. (Our strips measure 2×6 inches.)Adhere the ends of the strips with strong tape adhesive.
2. Cut circles from matching cardstock. Cut a short strip of cardstock and notch one end with scissors like a banner. Adhere to the back side of the circles, then adhere the circles to the napkin ring with strong tape adhesive.
3. Adhere a holiday die cut or punched piece to the circles. Embellish as desired.

For vase and place card containers
(1 large, 2 small)

1. Cut strips of cardstock/patterned paper to fit around vases. Adhere with strong tape adhesive. Fill large vase with beads or mini ornaments.
2. Embellish small containers with die-cut or punched holiday shapes, twine, and ribbon. Place a votive candle in each small container. **Note:** Be sure that any ribbon or twine is kept away from flame.

Never leave a burning candle unattended.

Whether you prefer an herbal green tablescape or a sweet candy cane-inspired place setting, your guests will love your holiday table.

Herbal Place Setting

Fresh-cut herbs add a perfect aroma and holiday green to your Christmas table setting.

WHAT YOU DO

Choose a natural-color tablecloth and dishes in deep green colors. Make a wreath of rosemary by twisting the fresh herb around a wire, twisting to hold at the ends. Slide the napkin through the little rosemary wreath. Fill small bottles with fresh herbs such as basil, parsley, and rosemary and use as table favors or centerpieces.

Sweet Candy Tablescape

All shades of pink combine to make a sweet sugarplum fairy look for this casual table setting.

WHAT YOU DO

Choose a pink polka-dot tablecloth. Layer white and pink dishes. Fold a pink-striped napkin into fourths. Cut a strip of print scrapbook paper and wrap around the napkin. Add a purchased alphabet sticker to the front. Fill a glass with candy canes for a table favor or centerpiece.

Add dramatic flair to your Christmas table by using black and white polka dots and stripes. Or choose nature's neutral colors and textures for a calming holiday tablescape.

Beautiful Black and White

Black and white polka dots and striped ornaments make a fun and festive graphic tablescape.

WHAT YOU DO

Choose black and white dishes for this fun place setting. Each black napkin is wrapped with a scrapbook paper strip with self-adhesive letters to spell out a name. Add a bowl of black and white ornaments to complete the look.

Woodland Table Setting

Let nature inspire you when you plan your holiday table this year. Choose colors in warm browns and whites—then add texture with twigs and bark.

WHAT YOU DO

Start with dishes in warm neutral tones. Choose napkins with subtle texture and color. A birchbark basket holds creamy ornaments for a simple centerpiece. Personalize a purchased ornament with little twigs that form a letter.

Gingerbread Man Setting

Always a favorite motif, the gingerbread man will help you create this homespun setting for your holiday table.

WHAT YOU DO

Fold a piece of 3×18-inch brown kraft paper accordian-style. Trace the pattern, below, and lay the pattern on the folded paper with arms and legs on the fold. Cut through all of the layers. Cut enough garland to lay under all of the plates. Choose white plates and red-and-white checked napkins. Wrap a piece of green scrapbook paper around the napkin. Add a gingerbread man sticker, ribbon, and jingle bell.

Gingerbread Man Garland

Full-Size Pattern

Fold

Fold

Fold

Fold

Wrapped-Up Table Setting

Wrap each place setting as if you are presenting the best gift of all. Then add a centerpiece of a stacked tower of gifts adorned with a satin ribbon.

WHAT YOU DO

Choose square dishes that can be stacked such as a salad plate on a dinner plate. Using wide ribbon, wrap each set of dishes like a package. Add a name tag to the bow. For the centerpiece, wrap three graduated boxes in coordinating ribbon. Tie a bow around the three packages.

Stitch Diagrams

Backstitch

Chain Stitch

French Knot

Running Stitch

Star Stitch

Stem Stitch

Straight Stitch

Index

Tips for Felting Wool

Felting wool fabric brings the fibers in the wool closer together and gives it a more compact look and feel. The texture becomes more irregular and interesting. Always choose 100% wool fabric to felt. Sweaters that are nearly 100% wool will work, but the fibers will not be as tight. Sweaters that have less than 90% wool will not work well.

Place the wool inside an old pillowcase to prevent any tiny fibers from washing out. Then wash the wool in very hot water with a little laundry detergent. Agitation of the wool loosens fibers and helps to shrink the wool. Dry the wool in a hot dryer to shrink the maximum amount.

Press the wool with a press cloth if desired. Tightly felted wool does not ravel, and edges and seams can usually be left raw or unfinished, similar to purchased felt.

Craft Designers

Dawn Anderson • Heidi Boyd • Sonja Carmon • Carol Field Dahlstrom • Phyllis Dobbs • Katie LaPorte • Janet Pittman • Janet Petersma • Jan Teymeyer • Ann E. Smith • Alice Wetzel

Sources

Snowflake Charm—beadsmith.com
Beads—thebeadmonkey.com
Felt—woolfelt.com
Bird Clips—blumchen.com
Santa Boot—blumchen.com
Paint—deltacreative.com, plaidonline.com
General Crafting Supplies—hobbylobby.com, michaels.com
Paper/Scrapbooking Supplies
americancrafts.com, bazzillbasics.com
Paper tape/ribbon—cutetape.com